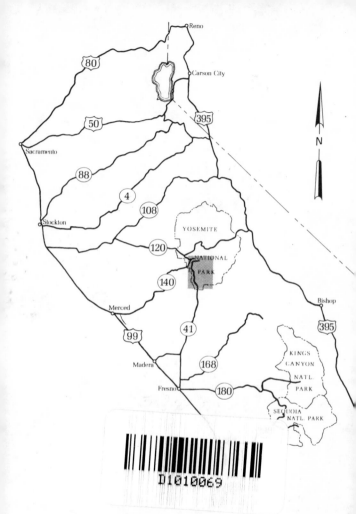

Location of the YOSEMITE quadrangle

This book is affectionately dedicated to Kris Kniffin

High Sierra
Hiking Guide

YOSEMITE

**a complete guide
to the Valley
and surrounding uplands,
including descriptions of
more than 150 miles of trails**

Jeffrey P. Schaffer

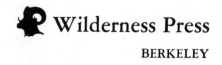

Wilderness Press

BERKELEY

Acknowledgments   I would like to thank Ron Mackie, Jr., Yosemite's Chief Backcountry Ranger, for reviewing the fourth-edition manuscript. Almost all of this book is a condensed version of part of my Yosemite National Park guidebook, and in the "Acknowledgments" of that book I list additional people who aided me on that project.

Photographs, maps and design by the author
Topographic maps revised and updated by the author,
    based on U.S. Geological Survey maps

Library of Congress Card Catalog Number 84-52659
International Standard Book Number 0-89997-052-4

Manufactured in the United States of America

Published by Wilderness Press
              2440 Bancroft Way
              Berkeley, CA 94704
              Write for free catalog

Library of Congress Cataloging in Publication Data

Schaffer, Jeffrey P.
   Yosemite : a complete guide to the Valley and
surrounding uplands, including descriptions of
more than 150 miles of trails.

   (High Sierra hiking guide ; 1)
   Condensed ed. of: Yosemite National Park. 2nd ed.
1983.
   Bibliography: p.
   Includes index.
   1. Hiking—California—Yosemite National Park—
Guide-books. 2. Trails—California—Yosemite National
Park—Guide-books. 3. Natural history—California—
Yosemite National Park—Guide-books. 4. Yosemite
National Park (Calif.)—Guide-books. I. Schaffer,
Jeffrey P. Yosemite National Park. II. Title.
III. Series.
GV199.42.C22Y6772   1985   917.94'47045   84-52629
ISBN 0-89997-052-4

Title Page: Lower Yosemite Fall

Contents

Introduction

THE WILDERNESS PRESS HIGH SIERRA HIKING GUIDES are pocket-size guides to the more popular parts of the Sierra Nevada proper. Each guide covers at least one 15-minute U.S.G.S. quadrangle, which is an area about 14 miles east-west by 17 miles north-south. The first page inside the front cover shows the location of the quadrangle covered by this guide.

In planning this series the editors used the 15-minute quadrangle as the unit because—though every way of dividing the Sierra is arbitrary—the quadrangle map is the chosen aid of almost every wilderness traveler. Inside the back cover is the author's updated topographic map of the quadrangle, which very accurately depicts the area's trails. With this map you can always get where you want to go, with a minimum of detours or wasted effort. (Additional copies of the map can be bought separately from Wilderness Press or its dealers.)

About two thirds of the trail description in High Sierra Hiking Guide #1 deals with trails in and about Yosemite Valley. Rightly called "The Incomparable Valley," it is a magnet that attracts visitors from all over the world. As John Muir noted long ago, the Sierra has several "Yosemites," though none of them matches Yosemite Valley in grandeur. Hetch Hetchy, to the north, is the foremost example of such a "Yosemite." Though some of these "Yosemites" rival or exceed Yosemite Valley in the depth of their canyons or the steepness of their walls, none has the prize-winning combination of its wide, spacious floor, its world-famous waterfalls, and its unforgettable monoliths—El Capitan and Half Dome.

The rest of the trail description deals with trails in a rather undramatic part of the Sierra Nevada. However, this description does include a network of trails through a grove of giant sequoias; no such trail system exists at the Park's two other groves. Although thousands of persons visit this area's Mariposa Grove each week during the summer, the vast majority ride the trams. The few who explore the grove on foot are richly rewarded.

Left: Yosemite Valley, viewed from Eagle Peak (Day Hike 11)

One very serious drawback to visiting this guide's area *in summer* is that then its lodges, hotels and campgrounds can't adequately handle all the visitors. To make *your* summer stay a pleasant one, be sure you make reservations well in advance. The Valley's lodges and hotels plus the Wawona Hotel are operated by the Yosemite Park and Curry Company, whose reservation desk you reach by phoning (209-252-4848). On private land in the Wawona area are The Redwoods (209-375-6256) and Camp Chilnualna (209-375-6295), which offer "cottages" with up to four bedrooms. Just outside the Park, near the start of the Glacier Point Road, is Yosemite West (209-372-4711, 372-4567, 372-6286), which offers condos and cottages. To camp in Yosemite Valley during the summer, you'd better make reservations with Ticketron (800-452-1111). They take reservations all year long. Campsites at our area's other campgrounds, Bridalveil and Wawona, are on a first-come, first-served basis. Finally, just below the Park's southern border is the USFS Summerdale Campground and the settlement of Fish Camp, with additional lodging.

You can get a copy of the Park's rules and regulations at one of its entrance stations. But there is one thing you ought to know before you leave home—don't take your pets. They are banned from the Park's trails and from most of the Valley's campgrounds.

Upper House, built in 1859, later converted to Cedar Cottage

The History

"THE GRANDEUR OF the scene was but softened by the haze that hung over the valley—light as gossamer—and by the clouds which partially dimmed the higher cliffs and mountains. This obscurity of vision but increased the awe with which I beheld it, and as I looked, a peculiar exalted sensation seemed to fill my whole being, and I found my eyes in tears with emotion." So wrote Dr. Lafayette Bunnell, a member of the Mariposa Battalion, of his group's discovery of Yosemite Valley on March 27, 1851. Today, many visitors seeing the Valley for the first time are struck with similar emotions.

The battalion entered the Valley in pursuit of a band of Ahwahnechee Indians under the leadership of Chief Teneiya. The Indians were captured, later released, and then decimated in 1853 by a band of Mono Indians. The Valley was now safe for tourists. James Hutchings was one of the earliest ones, and through his *Illustrated California Magazine,* the Valley became widely known. Roads, trails and hotels were built, guidebooks were written, and tourism increased. One important tourist was Frederick Law Olmsted, who visited the Valley and the Mariposa Grove of Big Trees in 1863 and noted that both were being ruined by commercial interests. He convinced U.S. Senator John Conness of California to introduce a park bill, which was subsequently signed by President Abraham Lincoln on June 30, 1864. The bill deeded the Valley and the Grove to California "for public use, resort and recreation."

But the lands surrounding these two tracts didn't fare well. Meadows were overgrazed by sheep (and to a lesser extent by cattle), and forests were depleted by loggers. This rape of the landscape was first noted by a young Scotsman, John Muir, who visited Yosemite Valley in 1868 and decided to stay. He explored the High Sierra and criticized its exploitation, but his protestations fell on deaf ears until 1889, when he met Robert Underwood Johnson. This editor of the very influential *Century Magazine* was impressed with both Muir and the High Sierra, and he had Muir write some Yosemite articles for his magazine. A park bill was introduced in Congress, and in October 1890, Yosemite National Park was created.

The bill, however, failed to stipulate how the Park should be administered. This task was given to the Army's Fourth Cavalry, which was stationed in Wawona. They stayed until the passage of the National Park Act of 1916, which established an administrative system for all the country's national parks and monuments. When the cavalry left Yosemite, they left behind an impressive record. They had driven sheep and cattle from the Park, had helped to settle property disputes, had laid the foundation for today's trail system, had mapped the Park in substantial detail and had even planted trout in the Park's lakes. For Yosemite, the cavalry had by and large "come to the rescue."

One serious incursion the cavalry was unable to prevent was the creation of Hetch Hetchy Reservoir, which lies about 15 miles northwest of Yosemite Valley. John Muir and his fledgling Sierra Club had fought a losing battle to defeat this San Francisco water project. To build a massive dam required lots of timber scaffolding, and 6+ million board feet of timber were logged *inside the Park* by the Yosemite Lumber Company. More than ½ *billion* feet of prime forest, including some of the Sierra's finest stands of sugar pines, were cut before 1930, when John D. Rockefeller, Jr. and the U.S. Government split the cost of buying up the logging company's interests. Today hikers can view part of the ravaged land—and walk along the company's abandoned railroad tracks—along Backpack Hike 2.

After World War II the Park's use greatly increased, and most of that use was confined to a small part of the Park—Yosemite Valley. The Valley was being loved to death. Beginning in 1970, the Park Service took steps to reduce the human impact in the Valley by instigating a shuttle-bus system, by reducing the number of campers and lodgers, by moving the sewage-treatment plant outside the Valley and by building bicycle paths to encourage nonmotorized use. The long-term goal, still years away, is to completely ban the automobile from the Valley. But it can never be returned to the pristine condition seen by its first discoverers, the Ahwahnechee Indians.

The Geology

NO OTHER LOCALE IN the Sierra Nevada receives so much use as does Yosemite Valley, which lies in the northern part of the area covered in this hiking guide. Visitors usually aren't interested in the geology of the rest of the area which, for the most part, is rolling, generally granitic upland terrain. Instead it is the Valley which causes them to ponder Nature's wondrous handicraft.

Even early visitors speculated on the Valley's origin. Josiah D. Whitney, the first director of California's State Geological Survey, proclaimed in 1867 that Yosemite Valley had been formed by some kind of faulting. This subsidence theory neatly "explained" the angularity and verticality of Yosemite's walls as well as the very small amount of talus found at the bases of these walls. A year later John Muir, as a young, unknown naturalist, explored the Yosemite area and concluded that the Valley was glacier-carved. Muir continued his explorations and in the following year discovered a small, active glacier on Merced Peak, at the headwaters of the Merced River.

To settle the Valley's origin "for all time," the U.S. Geological Survey assigned François Matthes the highly desirable task of thoroughly exploring Yosemite Valley and adjacent highlands in order to arrive at the truth. He once and for all destroyed Whitney's view of a fault-formed valley, but he also showed that Muir had greatly overstated the role of glaciation. On the basis of his field work, Matthes estimated that when the last of the glaciers had left Yosemite Valley, they had deepened it by 1500 feet at its east end, below Half Dome, while at Bridalveil Meadow they had deepened it by only 500 feet. He believed that glaciers had transformed Yosemite Valley from a strongly winding, V-shaped river canyon to a slightly sinuous U-shaped glacier trough. However, as later evidence was to reveal, there is a lot more to Yosemite Valley than meets the eye.

Seismic surveys were undertaken to determine the depth and configuration of the bedrock floor beneath the Valley. The results, published in 1956, indicated that a granite floor was as much as

2000 feet below the Valley surface in the vicinity of the Ahwahnee Hotel. Matthes had proposed only 300 feet. It seems the glaciers had been more powerful than Matthes had realized. They were and they weren't. First of all, they were because they had cut a basin out of bedrock to a depth that was a full 3000 feet below the Valley floor's pre-glacial level. But then, just 4 miles upstream, in Tenaya Canyon, the cross section between Mt. Watkins and Clouds Rest is unmistakably V-shaped, so it would appear that glaciers had barely altered the canyon here.

Why should the bedrock of Yosemite Valley be excavated to a depth of 3000 feet while in other Sierra canyons the excavation was typically only a few hundred feet? The answer is that Yosemite Valley is unique, due to the size, spacing and alignment of its *joints*. Joints are large, often linear, usually parallel fractures in bedrock. Without the presence of an overabundance of joints near the Valley's east end, 3000 feet of excavation never would have occurred. Furthermore, Yosemite Valley has steep-sided walls because the location and shape of its walls are governed by the presence of vertical joints. Glaciers didn't make the walls vertical; their contribution was minor—the walls were already steep, due to vertical jointing, prior to glaciation. We should note here that the *spacing* of joints is also important. If joints are closely spaced, the rock is more easily attacked—witness Indian Canyon and the Rockslides. The enormous cliffs that stand vertically above the floor of Yosemite Valley are due to vertical joints being spaced widely apart.

To visualize the effect of joints in controlling the development of a landscape, drive up the Glacier Point Road and get a bird's-eye view of Yosemite Valley and environs. Your first stop should be at Washburn Point, from which you look directly across at Half Dome. Note that it is not really half of a dome, for it is rather symmetrical, the southeast face being almost as tall and as steep as the northwest face. The steepness of each face is in large part controlled by vertical, northeast-trending joints. These vertical joints were more closely spaced along the northwest face, and glaciers took advantage of this, cutting the face back by about 500 feet.

Tenaya Canyon and Half Dome, viewed from Glacier Point

Also from Washburn Point, you'll see Mt. Broderick and Liberty Cap, this pair of "domes" lying below and to the right of Half Dome. Both are bounded by vertical, northwest-trending joints. Repeated glaciation has substantially enlarged the joint that separates the two monoliths. The same joint plane that governs the southeast face of Liberty Cap also governs the cliff that Nevada Fall leaps over. Vernal Fall is also governed by a vertical joint, but it trends northwest, not northeast. If such vertical joints had been closely spaced, then glaciers would have been able to cut through them, creating cascades, not falls.

Before driving on to Glacier Point, look at Mt. Starr King, on the horizon east-southeast of you. It is rounded on all sides—a true dome, unlike most so-called domes. If it is so rounded, does that mean it is not controlled by joints? Not really. Mt. Starr King appeared on the Yosemite landscape about 50 million years ago, if not earlier. It was almost certainly bounded by vertical, intersecting joint planes, and back in its early days it may have looked somewhat like Mt. Broderick, below you, looks today. Time and erosion, however, have taken their toll, eroding faster at the edges than at the faces, and even faster at the corners than at the edges.

From Washburn Point drive down to Glacier Point. The 1200-foot dead-vertical cliff below you is joint-controlled, but the curving Glacier Point Apron, below it, lacks major joints. From Glacier Point you can easily see how Half Dome got its name, for it certainly looks as if there had been a northwest half of the dome, which fell into Tenaya Canyon. Looking up Tenaya Canyon, we see that it is distinctly **V**-shaped in cross-section, not **U**-shaped, as a glaciated canyon is generally supposed to be. However, there are no major vertical joint planes in this canyon, so a **U**-shape never developed. Above the canyon stand North and Basket domes, both rounded like Mt. Starr King and both having a similar history.

We know that glaciers have entered Yosemite Valley for 2 million years, if not more. What we don't know, ironically, is when the *last* glacier left the Valley. The last major episode of glaciation in the Sierra Nevada is known as the Tioga stage, and it ended about 10,000 years ago. But were Tioga glaciers the last to enter Yosemite Valley or were some earlier glaciers the last? There are at least two views on this matter, and they center on a large lake that was supposedly left after glaciers retreated from the Valley.

Matthes envisioned "a mountain lake of exceptional beauty," 5½ miles long and 100–300 feet deep. The same seismic evidence that determined the depth of the Valley's sediments showed a buried layer that closely fitted Matthes' proposed lake. However, in 1976 the author calculated the volume of this supposed lake and its overlying sediments, and by determining the historic rate of sedimentation, he calculated that the Merced River and its tributaries would have required about 900,000 years to deposit these sediments. Clearly, then, a lake this size could not be filled in with sediments in the last 10,000 years, and therefore it would appear that such a lake existed before the Tioga stage; Tioga glaciers merely approached Yosemite Valley and dumped their sediments into it.

But there is an alternative interpretation. What if a massive Tioga glacier only slid over the Valley's sediments instead of ploughing deeply through them? Then, when it retreated, a shallow lake or a series of shallow lakes would have come into existence. If this happened, then it would have been entirely possible to fill the lake or lakes with sediments over the last 10,000 years. Not until we know just how deep the last Yosemite Valley glacier cut will we be able to complete our story on the origin and development of Yosemite Valley.

The Biology

WHO CAN FORGET HIS first visit to Yosemite—the enormous granite cliffs of El Capitan, the Cathedral Rocks, Half Dome and Clouds Rest, the leaping, dashing waterfalls, the smooth, glaciated domes of Yosemite Valley and Tuolumne Meadows, the lakes and high peaks? Of these features only the waterfalls move, and none are living. For most visitors, memories of living forms—except for giant sequoias—are likely to take a back seat to the inanimate landscape—although many out-of-state visitors will be duly impressed with the size of some conifers besides the sequoias. But despite the seemingly barren summits and cliffs, Yosemite is predominantly a landscape of forest green. Along most of this guide's trails, conifers shade our way.

The largest conifer in our area is, of course, the giant sequoia, which is the uncontested holder of the world heavyweight crown. But size hasn't always assured it success. In the past it was lucky just to survive its migration from Idaho. When southwest-migrating populations reached the area of the present Sierra Nevada about 10–15 million years ago, some encountered the volcanically active end of the Cascade Range, which back then extended as far south as Yosemite. Volcanic activity was particularly intense in the Tahoe area and northward, which explains why we don't see sequoia groves in the northern Sierra today. The northern immigrants were buried under lava flows and mud flows (this assemblage of volcanic rocks being collectively known as the Mehrten Formation). In more recent times the sequoia selected a habitat which is steadily being eroded away—a choice that could ultimately seal its doom. Furthermore, in order for its seeds to produce viable seedlings today, the sequoia grove depends on cone-boring cerambycid beetles, seed-eating Douglas squirrels and periodic ground fires. Remove any of these, and the future of the grove is in peril. (For more sequoia natural history, see Day Hike 25).

The sequoia grove is a miniature plant community, which, like our area's other plant communities, includes animals and microorganisms as well as plants. As in the sequoia community, the

Top left: cones of ponderosa pine (top), Douglas-fir (right) and sugar pine (bottom). Top right: cones of western white pine (left) and red fir (right). Bottom: white-fir branches (left) versus red-fir branches (right).

plants, animals and microorganisms in the other communities are regulated in number largely by their mutual interactions and by nonbiotic influences such as bedrock, soil, slope and microclimate. If you were to drive from Arch Rock Entrance Station up through Yosemite Valley and then up the Glacier Point Road to the Mono Meadow trailhead (Backpack Hike 4), you'd pass through a series of plant communities.

From the entrance station we'd be driving for miles mostly through a gold-cup-oak woodland, which locally can be dominated by Mariposa manzanita, as is true at the foot of El Capitan. If you were to walk through the woodland, you'd find it seemingly devoid of animals, save for the vociferous Steller's jays and pileated woodpeckers. But the animals are there. For example, look who feeds on whom. The oak's roots are tapped by root fungi, which are grazed by flat bugs and carrion beetles, which are eaten by western skinks (lizards), which are preyed upon by gopher snakes, which are seized by mountain king snakes, which are carried away by red-tailed hawks. And I've failed to mention hundreds of other interacting species. Incidentally, in this gold-cup-oak woodland, which does best on talus slopes, you are more likely to encounter rattlesnakes than in any other Yosemite community.

As you drive on toward Bridalveil Fall, you pass through a mixed-conifer forest, dominated by ponderosa pine, incense-cedar, white fir and Douglas-fir (not a true fir). Gold-cup oaks have been replaced by black oaks and, correspondingly, California ground squirrels have been replaced by western gray squirrels.

The dense, shady forest is a stark contrast to Bridalveil Meadow and the Valley's other meadows. These meadows, like the large one at Wawona, have been greatly altered from their natural state. In the Valley, former residents lowered the water table to drain bogs, eradicated trees to improve views, and suppressed fires to save forests (this last idea was counterproductive). These actions changed the characteristics of the meadows although not so much as did the grazing by livestock and the associated, usually un-intentional, introduction of alien plants. Galen Clark, the Park's first guardian, noted that in the 30 years that had passed since the Valley had been given "protection," its luxuriant native grasses and flowering plants had decreased to only one-fourth of their original number.

We leave the Valley, drive west up to barren, glaciated Turtleback Dome, then head south up to a junction with the Glacier Point Road. Along this leg we pass occasional sugar pines, which represent remnants of a large zone of sugar pines. In western Yosemite over ½ *billion* board feet of timber—a lot of it sugar pine—was cut by the Yosemite Lumber Company before it was bought out in 1930.

On the Glacier Point Road we climb east, entering a prime red-fir forest before arriving at Badger Pass. We then trade this forest for a lodgepole-pine forest as we skirt flatlands in the Bridalveil Campground area. This rather sudden change in tree type is due to the flatlands' high water table; the lodgepoles embrace it, the red firs abhor it.

Where the road bends north, we reach the Mono Meadow Trail, which begins in a magnificent grove of mature red firs. The forest floor is very shady, so few plants grow on it. Some that do, such as the snow plant, derive part of their nourishment by tapping their roots into soil fungi. Visitors become aware of a solemn feeling within such a forest, similar to being in a Gothic cathedral. What we sense is the stillness, the quiet. With little plant life on the forest floor, there is a definite absence of scolding rodents and singing birds.

If you were to take the Mono Meadow Trail east to the Buena Vista Trail and follow that trail south, you'd climb into other communities. With elevation you'd note the addition of western white ("silver") pines, followed by snow-loving mountain hemlocks. The hemlocks, unfortunately, prolong the duration of snow cover, which is a nuisance to hikers but a boon to snow mosquitoes. Despite their universal damnation, these blood-suckers (the females, that is) do have a highly redeeming trait: they are major pollinators of Yosemite's wildflowers.

The Buena Vista Trail guides one to the Buena Vista Peak area, which lies in the subalpine realm. Plants up there tend to be dwarfish, for winter's driving, subfreezing winds are extreme at these elevations, and plants survive better buried under snow than protruding above it. As in lower plant communities, plant-animal interactions are important. Near the top of 9709-foot Buena Vista Peak—the highest summit in our area—grow dense clusters of whitebark pines. Where you see these pines, you'll see Clark's nutcrackers, which are large, gray relatives of jays. The nutcrackers thrive on the pines' seeds, and they bury caches of seeds to last them through the year. The birds will eat most of the seeds, but a few survive to give rise to more pines. Thus the birds help to perpetuate the clusters of whitebark pines, just as the Douglas squirrels, lower down, help to perpetuate the groves of giant sequoias.

The Trails

THIS GUIDEBOOK IS AIMED at hikers—day hikers in particular. But some of the book's trails are also used by equestrians, for you can go on horseback rides along the floor of Yosemite Valley or around the rolling hills of Wawona. And the serious equestrian can arrange a backcountry trip, perhaps up to Merced Lake High Sierra Camp. Also, there are bike trails, these in the eastern half of Yosemite Valley. If you don't want to bring your own bike, you can rent one. (There are three other kinds of "trails": vertical, aerial and ski. Vertical trails are, of course, routes up the Valley's steep, granitic walls. If you're tempted to try this sport, contact Yosemite Mountaineering for lessons. If you're an accomplished climber, check first with the Park Service for regulations and restrictions. Aerial trails are the paths taken by hang-glider pilots. Only the most qualified pilots are allowed to fly—contact the Park Service. And in winter, you can ski downhill at Badger Pass or cross-country in a variety of places. Again, check with the Park Service for cross-country routes, weather conditions and potential hazards.)

The hikes in this book are divided into two kinds: day hikes and backpack hikes. For the latter, you'll need a wilderness permit, which you should get in person either at the Valley Visitor Center or at the Wawona District Office. While getting a permit, ask about possible water contamination and bear problems along your proposed route. Obviously, there are two advantages to day hiking: you can carry safe drinking water and you don't have to worry about midnight visits by bears. The bears, incidentally, rarely molest hikers; mostly they, like ground squirrels, go after your food.

You'll note that each hike in this book has a grade: a number-letter combination. The numbers refer to each hike's *total* mileage, as follows: **1** 0–4.9 miles, **2** 5.0–9.9 miles, **3** 10.0–14.9 miles, **4** 15.0–19.9 miles, and **5** 20.0+ miles. The letters refer to the total elevation gain you must climb: **A** 0–499 feet, **B** 500–999 feet, **C** 1000–1999 feet, **D** 2000–3999 feet, and **E** 4000+ feet. The words *easy, moderate* and *strenuous* describe the difficulty of the hike, given the recommended time. Of course, you can decrease the difficulty of most hikes by taking longer to do them.

You'll see at the end of each trailhead description a **boldfaced** letter-number combination, which refers to the location of the trailhead on the map in the back of this book. This grid-reference aid is provided for those hikers not familiar with the layout of trails in this part of Yosemite National Park.

The trails are virtually snow-free from early July through mid-October, although down in Yosemite Valley and about Wawona, this period is considerably longer, from about early April through late November. When your trail is partly snowbound, you can usually still follow it due to the aid of ducks or blazes. Ducks are two or more rocks, arranged in an obviously man-made fashion, which are often placed along a trail where it traverses bedrock. Blazes are obviously man-made scars cut in trailside tree trunks. They are usually in the shape of an **i** or a **T.**

If you want to see wildflowers at their prime, which unfortunately is at prime mosquito time, then visit the lower trails in May or June and the higher trails in June or July. If you're after a refreshing dip in a backcountry lake, in the Valley's Merced River or in Wawona's South Fork Merced River, then visit in early August, when the water temperature usually is at its maximum.

Of course, many people visit Yosemite Valley to see its waterfalls, which are at their best from mid-May to mid-June. You will, however, want to avoid visiting on the Memorial Day weekend when, as on the Fourth of July and the Labor Day weekends, the Park is severely overcrowded. For solitude, try visiting the Valley or Wawona in October or November, after the summer crowds have left and before the winter skiers have arrived.

That first impression of the Valley—white water, azaleas, cool fir caverns, tall pines and stolid oaks, cliffs rising to undreamed-of heights, the poignant sounds and smells of the Sierra ... was a culmination of experience so intense as to be almost painful.
                                                          —Ansel Adams

Day Hike 1
Valley Floor, West Loop

Distance: 6.9 miles (11.1 km) loop trip

Grade: 2B, easy half-day hike

Trailhead: Bridalveil Fall parking lot, 120 yards before the descending Wawona Road reaches a junction on the floor of Yosemite Valley. **C1.**

Introduction: This is the first of six Yosemite Valley floor hikes in this book, which are arranged from west to east. On this first loop hike you'll see Bridalveil Fall, the Cathedral Rocks and El Capitan all at close range.

Description: You could start this loop from Fern Spring, Bridalveil Meadow, Bridalveil Moraine, El Capitan Meadow or Devils Elbow, but we're starting from the Bridalveil Fall parking lot, since it has the most parking space. From the lot's east end you hike just two minutes on a paved trail to a junction, veer right and parallel a Bridalveil Creek tributary as you climb an equally short trail up to its end. During May and June, when Bridalveil Fall is at its best, your trail's-end viewpoint will be drenched in spray, making photography from this vantage point nearly impossible. Early settlers named this fall for its filmy, veil-like aspect, which it has in summer after its flow has greatly diminished. However, their predecessors, the Miwok Indians, named it *Pohono,* the "fall of the puffing winds," for at low volume its water is pushed around by gusts of wind.

After descending back to the trail junction, we quickly encounter three branches of Bridalveil Creek, each churning along a course that cuts through old rockfall debris. Keeping right at a trail junction, we follow our broad trail—the old Wawona Road until 1933— almost to the Valley's eastbound road, then quickly angle right to climb up to the crest of Bridalveil Moraine. From it we get a good view of the loose west wall of Lower Cathedral Rock and also the overhanging west wall of Leaning Tower.

Bridalveil Fall, or *Pohono*, the fall of the puffing winds

Just past the moraine's crest we enter a gully lined with big-leaf maples, and here we have an excellent head-on view of mammoth El Capitan. Then, only yards away from the base of the forbidding north face of Lower Cathedral Rock, we can stretch our necks and look up at its large ledge, covered with gold-cup oaks, that almost cuts the face in two. We continue east through a conifer forest, soon crossing a narrow, open talus field. At its base stands a second moraine, similar to Bridalveil Moraine, and both probably were left where a receding glacier temporarily halted its retreat.

Walking among white firs, incense-cedars, ponderosa pines, Douglas-firs and black oaks, we continue on a generally view-impaired route to a brief climb almost to the base of overwhelming Middle Cathedral Rock, and here you'll find it worth your effort to scramble 50 yards up to the actual base. Touching the base of this rock's overpowering, 2,000-foot-high, monolithic face can be a humbling experience.

Beyond the massive northeast face and its two pinnacles, we gradually descend to a level area, from which you could walk north-west a bit to a turnout on the eastbound road. From that turnout you can plainly see the two Cathedral Spires. These spires, and the 500-foot-high buttress they stand on, resemble a two-towered Gothic cathedral—hence the name. Despite their apparent inaccessibility, both were first climbed way back in 1934, during the early days of Yosemite Valley rock climbing.

About a one-third-mile walk beyond the level area we arrive at a signed trail, veer left on it, and descend to a point on the eastbound road only 20 yards west of the Cathedral Picnic Area entrance. The few people who head north to the picnic area will be rewarded with two classic views, one of El Capitan and another of the Three Brothers. Our route, however, continues northwest almost to a bend in the Merced River, from which you are bound to see—at least on summer days—sunbathers basking on the long, sandy "beach" of the far shore. Since our route eventually goes over to that vicinity, hikers with swimsuits on can shortcut across the wide, chest-deep Merced to that sunny beach. Non-swimmers follow the trail briefly west to the El Capitan Bridge. Here, by the eastern edge of El Capitan Meadow, the hiker gets reflective views of the Cathedral Rocks, and one can see why the Miwok Indians visualized the lower rock as a giant acorn.

From the El Capitan Bridge you walk north either along the road or its adjacent riverbank trail to a sharp bend. By continuing east about 250 yards you can reach the extremely popular Devils Elbow Picnic Area. Not only does it have the finest "beach" in the Valley, but it also has a splendid mid-river rock that is perfect for diving.

At the river bend we cross the main road and start west along an old paved road that in ⅓ mile comes to a small hollow from whose north end a *de facto* trail climbs to the nose of El Capitan. For the visitor new to Yosemite Valley, the size of El Capitan, like the Cathedral Rocks and other Valley landmarks, is too large to really comprehend, and many visitors who first try to estimate its size swear it is only 1000 or so feet high.

Beyond this vicinity our road rolls gently west to a junction with a trail, but we stick to our closed road and quickly reach the main road at the west end of El Capitan Meadow. After Yosemite became a national park in 1890 El Capitan Meadow became the Valley's first free public campground and Bridalveil Meadow soon became the second. Three other campgrounds—all in the meadows—were soon operating, in contrast to the forested ones we have today. Back then, horse pasturage was a prime concern— hence the need for meadow sites.

Leaving the meadow's edge you walk briefly west along the paved road and cross two usually dry branches of Ribbon Creek. In ¼ mile we come to a dirt road, and by walking just a few paces up it we immediately reach a westbound trail. After walking about five minutes west on it we cross a low recessional moraine, then drop almost to the paved road's edge. Here a turnout provides drivers and us with an unobstructed view of Bridalveil Fall. Under the pleasant shade of ponderosa pines and incense-cedars we continue west, passing some cabin-size rockfall blocks immediately before skirting the north end of the Bridalveil Meadow moraine. Soon we enter a swampy area with cattails and at its west end cross trickling Black Spring. Past the spring our trail more or less parallels the westbound road, shortly arriving at the back side of the Valley View scenic turnout. Here we see El Capitan, Bridalveil Fall and the Cathedral Rocks magnificently standing high above the stately conifers that line Bridalveil Meadow. Barely rising above the trees are the distant landmarks of Clouds Rest, Half Dome and Sentinel Rock.

From the Valley View area we reach our trail's westernmost point at the Pohono Bridge, which is the current ending point of north-valley one-way traffic. From a stream-gaging station across the bridge our feet tread a riverside path past popular roadside Fern Spring, then past generally unknown trailside Moss Spring. Pacific dogwoods add springtime beauty to this forest as sunlight filters down to light up their translucent leaves and their large, petal-like, creamy-white bracts. Douglas-firs locally dominate the forest as we hike through it to Bridalveil Meadow. Here you walk northeast along the road's side, staying above seasonally boggy Bridalveil Meadow. By the meadow's edge, the trail resumes, and it goes north to a bend, where you cross the Bridalveil Meadow moraine. From here one can walk 40 yards north to a large rock by the Merced River's bank and see a plaque dedicated to Dr. Lafayette Bunnell, who was in the first-known party of white men to set foot in Yosemite Valley.

From the moraine we parallel the Merced River southeast almost to the paved two-way road, which you can take ¼ mile east back to the Bridalveil Fall parking lot. Doing so in springtime avoids the possibility of getting your feet wet in the nearby fords of multibranched Bridalveil Creek. After the last ford the trail parallels the creek's northern branch east about 300 yards to the Valley's eastbound road. Here you can head southwest on it to the parking lot or walk northeast 200 yards to a resumption of the trail, on which you then head southeast toward Bridalveil Fall, perhaps revisiting it as you retrace your last steps back to the lot.

Day Hike 2
Valley Floor, Yosemite Lodge Loop

Distance: 7.0 miles (11.3 km) loop trip

Grade: 2A, easy half-day hike

Trailhead: Yosemite Falls parking lot, which is immediately west of the Yosemite Creek bridge and immediately north of the Yosemite Lodge complex. **D1.**

North Dome, Clouds Rest and Half Dome, from Leidig Meadow

Introduction: Most of this loop is relatively quiet and lightly traveled. On it you'll get a classic view of the Three Brothers plus other less famous but equally dramatic views.

Description: Behind the restrooms at the west end of the Yosemite Falls parking lot you'll find a trail heading southwest. On it you almost touch the main road, then curve right to the base of Swan Slab, which is a low cliff that attracts many rock climbers. A little less than ½ mile from the falls' lot we reach the Yosemite Falls trail (**Day Hike 10**), then pass above Sunnyside Campground, a walk-in, no-reservation campground heavily patronized by rock climbers. The trail turns south and descends—obscurely in times past—along the campground's west edge.

You next cross the paved, one-way road and on a trail parallel it southwest. In about a minute you may see a trail, branching southeast. This unofficial path goes across the west edge of grassy Leidig Meadow to a sandy beach beside the Merced River, and then parallels it about ½ mile upstream to a long, sturdy bridge that spans this river. From the west edge of the meadow you get one of the Valley's best views of North Dome, Royal Arches, Washington Column, Clouds Rest and Half Dome. Partly obscuring Half Dome is a large descending ridge on whose dry slopes the Four Mile Trail (**Day Hike 17**) zigzags down from Glacier Point. Looking west from Leidig Meadow, you get a clear view of the Three Brothers, named for three sons of Chief Teneiya who were taken prisoner here in May 1851 by the Mariposa Battalion. The vertical east face of Middle Brother was the origin of a March 1987 rockfall that left most of the rocky debris you are about to cross.

Back on the main trail we find that it is now confined to a narrow strip of vegetation between the busy, paved road above us and the silent river at our feet. Light-colored, giant boulders from the '87 rockfall contrast with darker, lichen-covered ones of former rockfalls. Soon we leave the river's side and parallel the road at a short distance, hiking through a forest of pine, incense-cedar and oak. After a mile of pleasant walking along the trail, part of it with fair views, we arrive at the El Capitan Picnic Area. Our route leaves this area as an abandoned road and then in ⅓ mile we enter a meadow and have good views of many of the Valley's prominent features, particularly looming El Capitan, the angular Three Brothers and the domed Cathedral Rocks. Beyond the meadow the trail skirts along the road and quickly reaches congested Devils Elbow Picnic Area. The area's fine beach and a superb sunbathing/diving rock in a swimming hole in the Merced River together account for the popularity. You'll find outhouses north of the picnic area's parking strip.

From the picnic area our trail quickly curves south, hugging both road and river for ¼ mile to the El Capitan Bridge, which is one of the Valley's most scenic spots (see **Day Hike 1**). At the north side of the bridge's east end the trail resumes, heads east to a bank opposite the south end of the Devils Elbow beach, then angles southeast to the eastbound Valley road. Just 20 yards east of us lies the entrance to the Cathedral Picnic Area and on its road we walk north down to the riverbank for two famous and instructive views. Looking northeast we note the amazing similarity among the Three Brothers. They present a classic case of joint-controlled topography. Each is bounded on the east and south by near-vertical joint planes and on the west by an oblique-angle joint plane. These three planes govern the shape of each brother.

Looking northwest we see the massive south face of El Capitan and on the east part of it identify the dark-gray "North America map," which is a band of diorite in a sea of granite.

Leaving the willow-lined Merced, we return to our trail, cross the road, and walk 250 yards southeast to a junction with the Valley's south-side trail. On it we start east and immediately cross a creek bed that is densely lined with young ponderosa pines. Looking upstream we see overhanging Taft Point, then get other views of it as we progress east. After ½ mile of shady, south-side walking, we come to a huge, trailside slab, on whose flat summit you'll find about 20 mortar holes used by the Indians to grind acorns to flour. Not a glacier-transported rock, this 1000-ton slab broke off a steep wall of the obvious side canyon above us. As we continue on, Douglas-firs and white firs mingle with the more dominant ponderosa pines, incense-cedars and black oaks.

Scattered views are obtained over the next mile from the big slab, and near its end we cross Sentinel Creek—barely a trickle on the first day of summer. After the summer solstice you're lucky if multistage Sentinel Fall, seen high above the creek, is even a gossamer mist. Voluminous only in flood stage, this fall is best seen in the warming days of late May.

After crossing the creek we come to an old spur road—the end of the Four Mile Trail from Glacier Point (**Day Hike 17**). In this vicinity Leidig's Hotel, the westernmost of several pioneer hotels, once stood. Beyond here our trail soon draws close to the Valley's eastbound road, and where we see a large roadside parking area, about ¼ mile beyond the old spur road, we leave our trail, cross the busy Valley road, and enter a picnic area. Black's Hotel once stood in this area, together with Clark's cabin. Galen Clark was one of the Valley's first tourists, and later became Yosemite's first guardian.

Descending through the picnic area we reach a long, sturdy bridge that replaces an earlier suspension bridge across the Merced River. From it you have good views of Yosemite Falls, Royal Arches, Washington Column, North Dome, Clouds Rest, Sentinel Rock, the Cathedral Rocks and the Three Brothers. From the far end of the bridge, two fishermen's paths start west, the right one skirting Leidig Meadow as it traces the river downstream. We take a broad, paved path north to a bend in the road on the grounds of Yosemite Lodge. Walk 100 feet along this bend to the path's resumption. It starts east, then curves north, finally crossing the Valley's one-way road by the main entrance to the lodge's grounds. This spot is also the west entrance to the Yosemite Falls parking lot, your starting point.

Day Hike 3
Valley Floor, Yosemite Village Loop

Distance: 3.3 miles (5.4 km) loop trip

Grade: 1A, easy 2-hour hike

Trailhead: Same as for Day Hike 2. **D1.**

Introduction: Famous views of Yosemite Falls, Half Dome and Royal Arches are seen along this short hike.

Description: While a steady stream of visitors make a short pilgrimage north to the base of Yosemite Falls, we walk southeast, bridge Yosemite Creek, then start east on a trail along the south side of the main road. Out trail quickly branches, and we angle right, away from the road to immediately cross a short spur road that heads south. Beyond the road our paved trail enters a beautiful, view-packed meadow, through which we start southeast but have the option to branch right, bridge the Merced River and head toward the Yosemite chapel.

By not branching right in the meadow, we end at a parking area with picnic tables, just north of Sentinel Bridge. Particularly during August, when Upper Yosemite Fall is only a wispy vestige of its springtime self, splashing children slowly raft down the river, adding a human element to the famous tree-framed view of stately Half Dome. By strategically locating their hotel in the area between this bridge and the chapel, Buck Beardsley and G. Hite in 1859 provided guests with the best of all possible views. Business, however, was poor, and in 1864 James Hutchings—one of the Valley's first tourists—bought the hotel.

From the south end of Sentinel Bridge we walk east on a paved riverbank trail, then cross the adjacent one-way road. Now we continue east beside the road, pass the bustling Housekeeping Camp, and soon arrive at a granite structure, the LeConte Memorial Lodge. It is named for Joseph LeConte, who was the first professor of geology at Berkeley's then-infant University of California. During the summer of 1870 he visited Yosemite Valley, met John Muir, and was profoundly impressed by both.

Leaving the LeConte Memorial and its trailside Indian mortar holes, we cross the road and follow a short path north along the east side of the Housekeeping Camp. In a few minutes we reach a sturdy bridge that links this camp to Lower Riverside Campground. Heading toward Yosemite Falls, we turn our backs on views of Glacier Point, the sweeping Glacier Point Apron and Grizzly Peak as we follow a path downstream, passing riverside alders and willows. Along this short stretch we note man's attempt to control nature: large granite blocks to prevent the river from meandering into either camp. Ponderosa pines, incense-cedars and black oaks provide shade until a small stretch of the Ahwahnee Meadow, just before the Valley's central road. In this small stretch our path crosses another one and heads straight toward Upper Yosemite Fall and, looking right, we have unobstructed views of North Dome, Royal Arches, Washington Column and Half Dome. Below these towering landmarks stands one of America's grandest hotels, the Ahwahnee, opened to the public in 1927.

After we cross the Valley's central road, we walk north, shaded by large black oaks growing along the edge of Ahwahnee Meadow. In ¼ mile we reach the west end of the Church Bowl, which has a paved roadside path and a dirt one, just behind the first, which we ascend northwest into the gold-cup oaks. Climbing from the Church Bowl up past the Lewis clinic, we quickly reach Indian Canyon Creek. Its canyon was a principal Valley exit used by the Indians heading up to the north rim, and early pioneers built a trail of sorts up to it, then west to a Yosemite Falls overlook. In early season you may note one of the Valley's lesser-known falls, Lehamite Falls, which plunges down a branch of Indian Canyon.

Beyond the canyon's creek and its huge rockfall boulders, we climb northwest to avoid a mosaic of Park buildings and residences, then contour west beneath sky-piercing Arrowhead Spire and the highly fractured Castle Cliffs. Approaching a spur trail down to the nearby government stables, we spy Lost Arrow—a giant pinnacle high on the wall of Upper Yosemite Fall. Heading west ¼ mile toward Lower Yosemite Fall, we come to a junction. From it you could take a trail down along Yosemite Creek to your trailhead, but then you'd miss this hike's best attraction, Yosemite Falls, whose base is just to the west. Along this ¼-mile stretch a sawmill once stood. It was located here because fast-flowing Yosemite Creek provided the water power necessary to turn the sawmill's large blade. John Muir built this sawmill for James Hutchings "to cut lumber for cottages . . . from the fallen pines which had been blown down in a violent windstorm [winter of 1867–68]."

From the bridge of Lower Yosemite Fall early-summer visitors are treated to the thunderous roar of the fall, a sound that reverberates in the alcove cut in this rock. During this season the visitor is further treated to the fall's spray as well. By late August, however, the fall, like its upper counterpart, is usually reduced to a mist, and even this can be gone by the Labor Day weekend. Dry or not, the fall should not be examined at close range, for even if boulder-choked Yosemite Creek is bone-dry, its rocks are water-polished to an icelike finish.

Before leaving the bridge, note how the lower fall has indirectly cut its alcove. Stream action has cut only a few feet into the granitic bedrock since glaciers last left the Valley, but in winter the fall's spray freezes in the surrounding rocks, expands, and pries loose lower slabs that in turn remove support from the upper ones—hence the rocky nature of Yosemite Creek's bed in this area. Walking back to your parking-lot trailhead, stop many times to get views of both falls. Long ago a swath of trees was logged just to provide these views.

Day Hike 4
Valley Floor, Camp Curry Loop

Distance: 2.8 miles (4.5 km) loop trip

Grade: 1A, easy 2-hour hike

Trailhead: Camp Curry parking lot, in eastern Yosemite Valley. **D1.**

Introduction: More like a stroll, this is the easiest hike described in this guide. It is recommended for those who enjoy a leisurely pace, and want to take the time to commune with the squirrels, birds and wildflowers and to reflect on the Valley's natural and human history.

Description: Back in the 1860s, long before a car entered Yosemite Valley, what is now the Camp Curry parking lot was an apple orchard, and rows of these fruit trees are still seen in the area today. From the southeast corner of Curry's lot we follow a paved path east past employees' tent cabins, then curve southeast and meet a short spur road that branches right. The open space it leads to used to be the site of the Camp Curry garbage dump, but the dump attracted so many bears that it was closed. From the south edge of this flat area, a five-minute climb along any of several paths up talus slopes will get you to the base of a broad, curving buttress known as the Glacier Point Apron. This relatively low-angle buttress is a very popular rock-climbing area, and until the 1980s most of its routes were quite difficult. However, with the advent of "sticky-soled" shoes, climbers found they could waltz up virtually any route. Consequently, new routes proliferated, unthinkable back in the 1970s.

From the spur road, our trail parallels the camp's road southeast to a nearby junction with a limited-access shuttle-bus road. About a minute's walk beyond it, we reach a trail branching right. Since this is a quieter route, we take it. It starts south, then rolls southeast, staying about 100–150 yards from the unseen shuttle-bus road, and in ⅓ mile intersects a southbound stock trail that links the Valley stables to the John Muir Trail. Beyond this intersection we head east on planks across a boggy area, and although mosquitoes may be bothersome in late spring and early summer, the bog does produce some nice wildflowers then. At a huge, lone boulder by the bog's east side, our trail angles southeast to several buildings in the Happy Isles area.

You'll probably see dozens if not hundreds of visitors in this area, and here you'll find an informative nature center, a curio shop and restrooms. Take some time to study the exhibits at the nature center and perhaps take in a show or a nature walk. Also visit the two Happy Isles, each surrounded by the splashing, joyously singing Merced River.

Departing north from Happy Isles, you have a choice of three pleasant routes: the Merced's west-bank trail, its east-bank trail, and the road's east-side trail. The east-side trail begins about 100 yards north of the gaging station, where it branches right, away from the east-bank trail. On the east-side trail you pass some cabin-size, moss-and-lichen-covered rockfall blocks, and then, where the trail climbs to cross the Medial Moraine, you descend across the road to the west-bending river. Both riverbank trails are relaxing strolls along the azalea-lined river, but perhaps the east-bank trail is more interesting since it traverses the base of west-trending Medial Moraine.

Skirting the south base of this moraine, the east-bank trail goes northwest almost to the Valley stables. Here, at the moraine's end, we turn left and immediately cross Clarks Bridge, named for Galen Clark, the Park's first guardian. From its west side those who took the Merced's west-bank trail now join us for a brief walk past the entrances to the Upper and Lower Pines campgrounds. Beyond them we meet a south-heading shuttle-bus road, but we turn right and walk west along a roadside trail to Stoneman Meadow and our parking lot trailhead.

Day Hike 5
Valley Floor, Mirror Meadow Loop

Distance: 3.6 miles (5.9 km) loop trip

Grade: 1A, easy 2-hour hike

Trailhead: Drive through the Pines campgrounds to road's end. Here, by a shuttle-bus stop just across Clarks Bridge, you'll find a parking lot beside the entrance to the Yosemite stables. **D1.**

Introduction: Shuttle buses once went to Mirror Meadow and Indian Caves, but now the paved road is used by bicyclists. Hikers too can use it, though paths offer quieter routes to these sites.

Description: The low ridge you see just behind the shuttle-bus stop is the Valley's "Medial Moraine," a glacial moraine whose origin is a matter of geological controversy. A trail goes east along each side of the moraine, the south-side trail being more scenic since it also goes along the Merced River. It is also quieter, for there are no trailside shuttle-buses. On this south-side trail we walk east along the base of the smooth moraine, leave the riverside trail, cross a shuttle-bus road from Happy Isles, and then continue east about 40 yards up to a north-south trail. Starting north on it we immediately top the moraine's crest, then descend northwest toward a road junction. The shuttle-bus route takes the road west, back toward our starting point, while bicyclists bound for Indian Cave or Mirror Meadow take the road north. Still on our trail, we meander north, skirting an area of large rockfall boulders that testify to the instability of Half Dome's west flank. Beyond the boulders we come to a trail intersection next to Tenaya Bridge. To cut your trip in half you could continue north from the bridge on a short trail to the Indian Caves trail, or to cut it even more, you could parallel the south bank of Tenaya Creek west back to the Yosemite stables. However, the described route turns right, starts east, and then parallels Tenaya Creek northeast up to a footbridge across that creek.

We cross the footbridge, climb briefly to the paved bicyclists' road, and head up it past a diminishing pond, which in the past lay just below the outlet of Mirror Lake. (By this pond is the start of a southwest-heading footpath, which is an alternate route back.) When you reach the road's end at what was once a parking area for autos and then a turnaround area for shuttle busses, you'll see that Mirror Lake exists no more. The lake used to dry up by late September, and at that time in past years the Park Service would excavate the lake, sometimes removing thousands of tons of sand and gravel. This material was later spread on snow-covered winter roads to make them more driveable. It was an efficient system. Environmentalists, however, thought otherwise, so the procedure was

Mirror Lake as it appeared in 1976

stopped, and after 1971 Mirror Lake began to silt up. Today, sand (and many Park employees) are transported to the Valley, expending wasteful amounts of fuel that add unnecessary carbon dioxide to an already-overladen atmosphere.

Today visitors must console themselves with Mirror Meadow, which in the late '80s was more gravely lake bottom than grassy meadow. However, by the turn of the century vegetation could cover all of the meadow—unless the lake's manmade dam is removed. This would lower the water table and allow trees to invade the meadow, ultimately obscuring all views.

To resume our loop hike, we look for a trail that starts near the back end of the former parking area. (Since this is a horse path and is heavily used, you might want to take the previously mentioned foot-path for a fresher-smelling route.) Starting south on the horse path, we see, high above, North Dome and Half Dome. Next, our trail passes myriad oversize boulders that came from the vertical east wall of Washington Column. Soon our trail switchbacks briefly down to the paved road, then goes 100 yards west to a trail departing south toward nearby Tenaya Bridge. Our trail continues west another 100 yards to enter the Indian Cave area. This area is a favorite spot for children, since dozens of caves can be found and dozens of house-size boulders can be climbed. However, if you have brought along children, please watch them closely. Before leaving this popular area, climb on top of a large, low slab that lies along the trail's north side. On its flat top you'll find mortar holes made by the Yosemite Indians and used by them to pulverize acorns.

Continuing west you have a choice: either stay on the trail or take the paved bike path, just south of the caves. The two diverge, and then, near the northeast corner of the Group Camp (old Camp 9), they come together. On this stretch you pass under the forbidding south face of Washington Column. Where the trail and the bike path come together, we can look up a deep cleft—eroded along a vertical fracture—which separates Washington Column from that giant lithic rainbow, Royal Arches.

After 150 yards of westward traverse our two parallel paths cross a very low moraine. About a two-minute walk past it we come to a trail junction, where, by cutting south through the Group Camp, one can save ⅓ mile. However, by continuing west for a few minutes along the bike path (the trail goes to the Ahwahnee Hotel), we reach the Sugarpine Bridge, named for a huge sugar pine growing by the northeast corner of the bridge. Like a royal arch, this stately giant could fall any day. From the bridge we take a trail first southeast up the Merced River, then briefly northeast up Tenaya Creek. Where we meet the southbound shortcut trail we take it, immediately bridge Tenaya Creek and walk southeast past the back side of North Pines Campground to the Valley stables.

Day Hike 6
Valley Floor, Tenaya Canyon Loop

Distance: 3.0 miles (4.8 km) loop trip

Grade: 1A, easy 2-hour hike

Trailhead: In lower Tenaya Canyon, at the end of the paved Mirror Meadow bike path (formerly, a shuttle-bus road). **D1-E1.**

Introduction: In addition to visiting the site of former Mirror Lake, you get ever-changing views of Half Dome and other features of deep, glaciated Tenaya Canyon.

Description: Before making this loop you'll want to descend a few steps to what was once Mirror Lake's most famous viewpoint. Visitors who have seen beautiful photographs of Mt. Watkins reflected in the lake's calm morning waters are due for a rude surprise. As elaborated in **Day Hike 5,** Mirror Lake, originally formed behind a rockfall and then artificially raised by a manmade dam, is now just a swampy meadow. Your loop trail begins at the lake's former parking area and quickly comes to the northwest arm of the former lake. About 100 yards beyond it, where the trail bends right, you may see a cliff with polish imparted by a glacier before it retreated up-canyon perhaps about 10,000 years ago. Unfortunately, a 1986 rockfall now prevents safe inspection of this polish.

Our trail leads us up-canyon under a shady forest cover, and soon we approach Tenaya Creek—a good picnic spot. Beyond it our trail rolls northeast toward the south spur of Mt. Watkins, which is occasionally seen through the forest canopy. About 1.1 miles from the trailhead we come to a junction to which a Tuolumne Meadows trail, with its nine dozen switchbacks, descends from Snow Creek. At most you'll want to ascend only the first dozen switchbacks, an effort sufficient to get you above the dense gold-cup oaks and present you with a view of Half Dome and much of Tenaya Canyon. The author believes that until only a few million years ago a major river flowed down this canyon, then the backward-cutting Tuolumne River diverted much of the drainage westward. Today, Tenaya

Creek is an underfit creek, one that dries up in late summer. From your vantage point in early summer, when the creek's flow is brisk, you ought to see Tenaya Creek falls, at about your elevation and about ½ mile up-canyon.

From the junction our canyon-floor trail again approaches the creek, and in ⅓ mile bridges it. Our return hike is along the east side of the creek, and it provides as pleasant a route as did our easy west-side route. About 1¼ miles from the creek's bridge we reach the east edge of Mirror Meadow, then soon stroll past its dam, an artificial feature built abound 1890 to add depth to the lake and to increase its photographic attributes. Just below the dam we descend to a pond that is gradually diminishing. In years past, it was one of the favorite swimming holes to be found in the Valley. Beyond the pond we leave the trail to Happy Isles, cross a footbridge and briefly walk up the paved bike path.

Day Hike 7
New Big Oak Flat Road to Cascade Creek

Distance: 7.8 miles (12.6 km) round trip

Grade: 2C, strenuous half-day hike

Trailhead: From Crane Flat drive east 6 miles toward Yosemite Valley down the new Big Oak Flat Road to the Foresta turnoff, on your left, then an additional ¼ mile to the first turnout with a Yosemite Valley view. Park there and walk back up to the Foresta road junction. **A1.**

Introduction: During the late spring, when most of Yosemite's trails are under snow, this trail is at its best. Views are few and lakes are nonexistent, so it will appeal only to those who want an invigorating yet not exhausting walk and to those who appreciate the finer details of mid-Sierran ecology.

Description: Our signed trail begins about 50 yards west of the Foresta road junction, and during spring you're likely to find a field of Stiver's lupines blooming in this vicinity. As we start our climb, gold-cup oaks quickly are replaced by incense-cedars, ponderosa pines and black oaks. After a 400-foot gain we top a ridge and from it we can see El Capitan and Half Dome to the east through the pines. These yield to white firs as we traverse north across slopes with deep, moist soils. About 1½ miles from the trailhead we descend to step across Wildcat Creek, which generally flows only through spring, then descend to hop two of its tributaries before climbing again. Along this shady stretch you're likely to see one or more passionate-red snow plants—a protected species.

About a mile past Wildcat Creek we reach a small ridge, see the Wawona Road on the flanks of Turtleback Dome, to the southeast, then immediately descend to long-lasting, fairly wide Tamarack Creek. Springtime visitors may have to wade across it. In the next mile we climb 500 feet, mostly under the shade of white firs, sugar pines and ponderosa pines.

After your trail finally levels out, it makes a brief drop to a Cascade Creek tributary, which is boulder hopped only yards away from the Old Big Oak Flat Road. At this creek crossing, service-berries hug the bank of a small pool fed by a splashing cascade. Once on the road, we have a brief walk down to the bridge across Cascade Creek—a good spot for a lunch break (camping prohibited). In late summer the flow of Cascade Creek is slow and warm enough for safe and enjoyable splashing around in the small pools immediately downstream. During the summer, when the road to Tamarack Flat Campground is open, you'll want to take the much shorter **Day Hike 8** down to Cascade Creek.

Day Hike 8
Tamarack Flat C.G. to Cascade Creek

Distance: 4.4 miles (7.1 km) round trip

Grade: 1B, easy half-day hike

Trailhead: From Crane Flat drive northeast 3¾ miles up Highway 120 to the Tamarack Flat Campground turnoff, immediately before the Gin Flat scenic turnout. Drive southeast down the Old Big Oak Flat Road to the east end of Tamarack Flat Campground, 3¼ miles from Highway 120. **A1.**

Introduction: Around mid-morning Tamarack Flat Campground becomes temporarily abandoned, only to receive another flood of motorized campers in late afternoon. Take the time to enjoy the campground during the tranquil part of day, and while you're in the vicinity, you might take a few hours to make this pleasant, easy hike.

Description: Some early visitors traveled by stagecoach to Yosemite Valley along this route, which was completed in 1874. About 100 years later visitors could still travel, by auto, from the campground down to Cascade Creek, but now the road is closed to motor vehicles.

Tamarack Flat derives its name from its extreme predominance of tamaracks, known today as lodgepole pines. However, as you leave the flats and hike across slopes on the Old Big Oak Flat Road, white firs become dominant. Along both sides of the road you'll see large, partly buried granitic boulders. These were not carried here by glaciers, instead, they developed right where you see them, being resistant enough to subsurface weathering that they finally emerged on the surface quite intact, while the adjacent, less resistant, more fractured bedrock was chemically broken down and slowly stripped away by erosion.

Just before you reach a prominent cluster of rocks your road begins a steady descent to Cascade Creek. At a road switchback just 240 yards before the bridge across this creek, you'll see a junction with a trail to the New Big Oak Flat Road, **Day Hike 7.** Along the first 200 yards below its bridge, Cascade Creek splashes down low

---

The clearest way into the Universe is through a forest wilderness.
—John Muir

cascades into small pools, and in late season these make nice "swimming holes." Before then the creek is likely to be too swift for safe frolicking. Rooted in this creek are large-leaved umbrella plants, and growing just beside the water's edge are creek dogwoods, willows, western azaleas and serviceberries.

Day Hike 9
El Capitan

Distance: 15.4 miles (24.8 km) round trip

Grade: 4D, strenuous day hike.

Trailhead: Same as for Day Hike 8. **A1.**

Introduction: The vertical walls of 3000-foot-high El Capitan attract rock climbers from all over the world, and about a dozen extremely difficult routes have been climbed up it. For nonclimbers this hike provides a much easier, safer way to attain El Capitan's summit, which stands only 15 feet above the north-side approach.

Description: Descend to Cascade Creek, as directed in **Day Hike 8,** then continue ½ mile down the Old Big Oak Flat Road—now more like a trail—to a junction with Yosemite Valley's north rim trail. Here a major climb of almost 2000 feet confronts us. Starting in a summer-warm forest, we climb hundreds of feet—steeply at times—up to drier slopes. We then encounter red firs, which grow near the top of the crest. Lodgepoles join in the ranks as we make a short descent from it down to a meadow, which guides us to a crossing of a Ribbon Creek tributary. This we parallel east 1 mile down to Ribbon Creek. Ribbon Meadow, which we traverse on the first part of this descent, is more forest than meadow, and, where the route becomes a little vague, blazes on lodgepoles guide you. Along the banks of Ribbon Creek are the trail's only acceptable campsites, for water runs down the creek until midsummer. Now only 1¼ miles from our goal, we make a brief climb, an equally brief descent, and then an ascending traverse east to the top of El Capitan Gully.

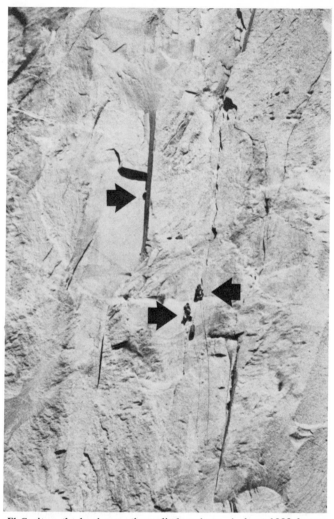

El Capitan, the hard way: three climbers (arrows) about 1000 feet up the monolith's prow

Your first views of El Capitan and the south wall of Yosemite Valley appear on this traverse to El Capitan Gully, and views continue as you climb south from the gully past dense shrubbery to a junction with the El Capitan spur trail. If you are hiking this trail in late summer, after Ribbon Creek has dried up, you may want to continue on the main trail ½ mile northeast to two trickling springs. The trail beyond them is not all that interesting, but it does get you to Eagle Peak (the long way) and to Yosemite Creek (see **Day Hike 11**).

Along the spur trail south to El Capitan's broad, rounded summit, you can gaze up-canyon and identify unmistakable Half Dome, at the valley's end, barely protruding Sentinel Dome, above the valley's south wall, and fin-shaped Mt. Clark, on the skyline above the dome. Take your time exploring El Capitan's large, domed summit area, but don't stray too far from it. Remember that many climbing deaths occur after the triumphant party has reached the summit.

Day Hike 10
Yosemite Falls

Distance: 6.6 miles (10.6 km) round trip

Grade: 2D, strenuous half-day hike

Trailhead: Park in the westernmost part of the Yosemite Lodge parking lot close to the gas station, which is on the north side of the main road. **C1-D1.**

Introduction: Most Park visitors walk to the base of Lower Yosemite Fall. This popular trail gets you to the other end—the brink of Upper Yosemite Fall. Like other early trails of Yosemite Valley, the Yosemite Falls trail was privately built and then was operated as a toll trail.

Description: From the gas station, pick any route along the east edge of Sunnyside Campground and then continue upslope a minute or so to the north-side Valley floor trail (**Day Hike 2**). By walking west on it for a minute or so, you should reach the start of the Yosemite Falls trail. We leave conifers behind as we start up nearly four dozen switchbacks. Characteristic of old trails, each switchback is short. Under the shade of gold-cup oaks, which dominate talus slopes like the one we're on, our so-far viewless ascent finally reaches a dry wash that provides us with framed views of Leidig Meadow and the Valley's central features.

With more than one fourth of the elevation gain below us, we pass by more oaks and an occasional bay tree as we now switchback east to a panoramic viewpoint, Columbia Rock, which is a worthy goal in itself. At its safety railing we can study the Valley's geometry, from Half Dome and the Quarter Domes west to the Cathedral Spires. Looking down on the Valley floor you might observe some old, abandoned meanders of the Merced River. A few gravelly switchbacks climb from the viewpoint, and then the trail traverses northeast, drops slightly, passes an enormous Douglas-fir, then bends north for a sudden dramatic view of Upper Yosemite Fall. West of the falls' lower section is a white scar 100 feet high, from which a 1,000-ton rock slab fell, after being struck by lightning in June 1976. In clear weather in November 1980, there was another major rockfall, which left a conspicuous scar on the cliffs west of and above the trail. Three hikers were killed. Another rockfall occurred nearby in July 1985. Other trails climbing out of the Valley have also experienced rockfalls—the Valley's walls aren't as eternal as they may appear.

Our climb up the long, steep trough ends among white firs and Jeffrey pines, about 135 switchbacks above the Valley floor. Here, in a gully beside a seasonal creeklet, our trail turns right while the Eagle Peak Trail, **Day Hike 11,** continues ahead. Our trail makes a brief climb east out of the gully and reaches a broad crest with several overused campsites. Their heavy use puts a strain on this area's vegetation, and it is best not to camp here. Along the crest we follow a trail south almost to the Valley's rim; then at a juniper we veer east, descend steps almost to Yosemite Creek and finally descend more steps to a fenced-in viewpoint. If you're acrophobic you should not attempt the last part of this descent, for it is possible,

Upper Yosemite Fall, from about switchback 89

Lost Arrow spire, first climbed in 1946

though unlikely, that you could slip on loose gravel and tumble over the brink. Beside the lip of Upper Yosemite Fall we see and hear it plunge all the way down its 1430-foot drop to the rocks below. Just beyond the fall is a large roof, and beyond it stands the pride of the Clark Range, finlike Mt. Clark.

After returning to the crest campsites you can descend east to a bridge over Yosemite Creek and obtain water. However, be careful! Almost every year one or more persons, wading in the creek's icy water, slip on the glass-smooth creek bottom and are swiftly carried over the fall's brink. From the creek's bridge you could continue eastward ¾ mile up a trail to Yosemite Point. From that viewpoint a dramatic panorama extends from Clouds Rest south past Half Dome and Glacier Point, then west to the Cathedral Rocks. Near you a massive shaft of rock, Lost Arrow, rises almost to the Valley's rim, and beyond it you can see most of the switchbacking Yosemite Falls trail. See the *Hetch Hetchy* High Sierra Hiking Guide for trail description north from this viewpoint.

Day Hike 11
Eagle Peak

Distance: 12.4 miles (20.0 km) round trip

Grade: 3E, strenuous day hike

Trailhead: Same as for Day Hike 10. **C1-D1.**

Introduction: Strategically located Eagle Peak, highest of the Three Brothers, provides commanding views both up and down Yosemite Valley. The hike to it also provides exciting views, including some close-range ones of Upper Yosemite Fall.

Description: Follow **Day Hike 10** up to the Upper Yosemite Fall fenced-in viewpoint, then return to the trail junction in the gully west of the fall. From it we begin a shady trek north, climbing out of our gully, descending into a second and climbing out of a third to a trail junction. Leaving the Yosemite Creek environs, we climb more than 300 feet, at first steeply, before leveling off in a bouldery area—part of a moraine. This moraine marks the southernmost extent of a glacier that descended from the west slopes of Mt. Hoffmann. Now we turn south, generally leaving Jeffrey pines and white firs for lodgepole pines and red firs as we climb to Eagle Peak Meadows, whose north edge is blocked by an older moraine.

Beyond the sometimes boggy meadow we cross the headwaters of Eagle Peak Creek and in a few minutes reach a hillside junction. From it an old trail climbs and drops along a 1¾-mile course to the El Capitan spur trail. To reach the summit of that monolith, it is easier to start from Tamarack Campground (**Day Hike 9**). From the junction we branch left for a moderate ⅔-mile ascent to the diminutive summit of Eagle Peak. From the weather-pitted, brushy summit 3200 feet above the Valley floor, we get far-ranging views that extend all the way to the Sierra crest along the Park's east boundary. Below us central Yosemite Valley spreads out like a map, and you should be able to identify most of its major landmarks.

Day Hike 12
Wawona Tunnel to Dewey Point

Distance: 10.9 miles (17.5 km) round trip

Grade: 3D, moderate day hike

Trailhead: Discovery View, at the east end of Wawona Tunnel, on the Wawona Road 1.5 miles west of the Bridalveil Fall parking lot entrance. **B1.**

Introduction: Five viewpoints are visited: Inspiration, Old Inspiration, Stanford, Crocker and Dewey. The first two, however, are somewhat blocked by vegetation. By hiking only to Stanford Point, you cut about 2½ miles and 900 feet of climbing from your hike. The creeks found along this route typically dry up by early summer so make sure you bring enough water.

Description: Our signed trail starts at the west end of the south-side parking lot and makes a switchbacking, generally viewless 500-foot ascent for 0.6 mile up to an intersection of the old Wawona Road. Constructed in 1875, this old stage route got a lot of use before it was closed with the opening of the newer Wawona Road in 1933. Today it provides a quiet descent 1.6 miles down to the newer road, meeting it just ⅓ mile above the entrance to the Bridalveil Fall parking lot.

Beyond the intersection our oak-and-conifer shade stays with us all the way up another 500-foot ascent, keeping us cool but also hiding most of the scenery. At Inspiration Point we meet a bend in the old Wawona Road, a point where early travelers got their first commanding view of El Capitan, Bridalveil Fall and the Cathedral Rocks. Today incense-cedars, oaks and pines obstruct the view.

With most of our climb still ahead of us, we push onward, winding up 1200 vertical feet of the Pohono Trail before arriving at springtime-active Artist Creek. Now at an elevation with cool rather than warm afternoon temperatures, we make a steep 300-foot climb to signed Old Inspiration Point, whose view is in part blocked by a large sugar pine.

Red firs now add shade to the forest canopy as we briefly ascend before dropping to a welcome spring and nearby Meadow Brook. If any water remains along this trail through mid-summer, it will be found here. Beyond the creek and its alders we head north and soon descend to our first significant viewpoint, at the end of a short spur trail—Stanford Point. From it we see the gaping chasm of western Yosemite Valley and we identify easily it prominent landmarks: Leaning Tower, Bridalveil Fall, the Cathedral Rocks, El Capitan and, seasonally, Ribbon Fall. Excited by this stunning panorama we climb ½ mile farther, reaching Crocker Point after more than 400 feet of elevation gain. Crocker Point, standing at the brink of an overhanging cliff, provides a heart-pounding view similar to the last one, though better. Now most of the Valley's famed landmarks stand boldly before us and we look over all the Cathedral Rocks to see the Three Brothers. To the left of Clouds Rest we see twin-towered Cathedral Peak and broad-topped Mt. Hoffmann, with distant Mt. Conness between them, marking the Sierra crest along the Park's northeast boundary.

After the Crocker Point revelation, can we expect anything better? You'll have to judge for yourself after continuing ⅔ mile to Dewey Point. Now closer to the Cathedral Rocks, your perspective is different and you look straight down the massive face that supports Leaning Tower. Also intriguing is the back side of Middle Cathedral Rock, whose iron-rich, rust-stained surface stands out among the rest of the Valley's gray, somber colors. Finally you see the Cathedral Spires head-on so they appear as one. After scanning the Valley and the horizon, leave the point and descend the way you came.

Day Hike 13
Bridalveil Campground to Dewey Point

Distance: 10.0 miles (16.1 km) round trip

Grade: 3C, moderate half-day hike

Trailhead: From Chinquapin Junction on the Wawona Road, drive 7.6 miles up the Glacier Point Road to the Bridalveil Creek Campground spur road. Turn right and drive 0.5 mile to the campground's entrance. **C2.**

Introduction: This is the easier of two routes to scenic Dewey Point and it requires less than half the climbing effort of the previous hike, but then it doesn't visit Stanford and Crocker points.

Description: At the entrance to Bridalveil Campground a closed road departs southwest away from the camp's Loop A. On it we soon cross a creek that drains Westfall Meadows, then immediately meet a trail. Heading south, this undesirable trail passes through these meadows, then makes a brush-choked descent to an old logging area—a 1920's "battleground" between environmentalists and the Yosemite Lumber Company. The environmentalists won, but the scars remain.

Rather than head south we take a trail north, which climbs gently over old, weathered terrain to the Glacier Point Road. By starting here—¼ mile west of the campground's spur road—you could knock 1¾ miles off your total distance. From the road our lodgepole-shaded route gently descends almost to the north tip of largely hidden Peregoy Meadow before topping a low divide. Next we drop moderately and reach a small cabin near the south edge of McGurk Meadow. A small footbridge in it takes us across the creek that drains this sedge-rich, sometimes flowery meadow.

From the meadow we see the low summits of the Ostrander Rocks to the east and then at the meadow's north end re-enter dense lodgepole forest. Our trail soon crests at a shallow, viewless saddle, then descends moderately to gently to a low-crest trail fork. The fork right quickly joins the Pohono Trail and drops to a campsite alongside Bridalveil Creek. We fork left, quickly join the Pohono Trail, start west on it and, near a broad, low divide, traverse a dry, gravelly slope.

The forest cover now becomes dominated by firs, and on the damp shady floor beneath them you may find wintergreen, snow plant and spotted coralroot, the last two being saprophytes. Two Bridalveil Creek tributaries are crossed, then a smaller third one before we start up a fourth that drains a curving gully. On the gully's upper slopes Jeffrey pine, huckleberry oak and greenleaf manzanita replace the fir cover and in a few minutes we reach highly scenic Dewey Point, described at the end of **Day Hike 12.** If you can get someone to meet you at the Wawona Tunnel, then descend to it along this highly scenic portion of the Pohono Trail.

Day Hike 14
The Fissures at Taft Point

Distance: 2.6 miles (4.1 km) round trip

Grade: 1A, easy 2-hour hike

Trailhead: From Chinquapin junction on the Wawona Road, drive 13.2 miles up the Glacier Point Road to a scenic turnout, on your left, which is 2.3 miles before the Glacier Point parking-lot entrance. **D1.**

Introduction: The views from Taft Point rival those from Glacier Point. However, since Taft Point is reached by trail, it is sparsely visited compared to Glacier Point. Generally lacking protective railings, Taft Point and the Fissures are potentially dangerous, so don't bring along children unless you can really keep them under strict control.

Description: From the road-cut parking lot we descend about 50 yards to a trail, turn left, and start southwest on it. After about 150 yards of easy descent we pass a trailside outcrop that is almost entirely composed of glistening whitish-gray quartz. It also has small amounts of pink potassium feldspar. In a minute we come to seasonal, murmuring Sentinel Creek, whose limited drainage area keeps Sentinel Fall downstream from being one of Yosemite Valley's prime attractions. After boulder-hopping the creek we follow an undulating trail west past pines, firs and brush to a crest junction with the Pohono Trail. Just north of it you'll notice some

Sentinel Dome's lone Jeffrey pine, as it appeared in 1976

large, weathered boulders. Not left by glaciers, these boulders weathered in place and will continue to "grow" as the surrounding bedrock is stripped away.

From the junction we descend to a seeping creeklet that drains through a small field of corn lilies. Descending toward the Fissures, we cross drier slopes that are generally covered with brush. Soon you arrive at the Fissures—five vertical, parallel fractures that cut through overhanging Profile Cliff, beneath your feet. Beyond the Fissures we walk up to a small railing at the brink of a conspicuous point and get an acrophobia-inducing view of overhanging Profile Cliff, beneath us. For the best views of Yosemite Valley and the High Sierra walk west to *exposed* Taft Point, from where you see the Cathedral spires and rocks, El Capitan, the Three Brothers, Yosemite Falls and Sentinel Rock. Broad Mt. Hoffmann stands on the skyline just east of Indian Canyon and east of that peak stands distant Mt. Conness, on the Sierra crest.

Day Hike 15
Sentinel Dome

Distance: 2.4 miles (3.9 km) round trip

Grade: 1B, moderate 2-hour hike

Trailhead: Same as for the Hike 14 trailhead. **D1.**

Introduction: Sentinel Dome is perhaps the most-climbed dome in the Park. Lembert Dome and Pothole Dome, both in the Tuolumne Meadows area, may be climbed more often, but neither is a true dome but rather each is a *roche moutonnée*—an unsymmetrical glacier-formed feature.

Description: From the road-cut parking lot we descend about 50 yards, turn right and make a curving, generally ascending traverse ¾ mile north almost to the south base of Sentinel Dome. Here we meet and briefly hike north on a road, then come to a fork, where we veer left, and in 30 yards, at another fork, we veer left again. In a few minutes we arrive at the dome's north end, where we meet a path from Glacier Point. We now climb southwest up a bedrock route to the summit. Though a real trail up to it doesn't exist you should have no problems getting there.

At an elevation of 8122 feet, Sentinel Dome is the second highest viewpoint above Yosemite Valley. Only Half Dome—a strenuous hike—is higher. Seen from the summit, El Capitan, Yosemite Falls and Half Dome stand out as the three most prominent Valley landmarks. West of Half Dome are two bald features, North and Basket domes. On the skyline above North Dome stands blocky Mt. Hoffmann, the Park's geographic center, while to the east, above Mt. Starr King (another dome) stands the rugged crest of the Clark Range. In the past almost everyone who climbed the dome expected to photograph its famed, windswept, solitary Jeffrey pine. This tree, unfortunately, finally succumbed to vandalism in 1984.

Day Hike 16
South Rim Traverse

Distance: 13.5 miles (21.7 km) one way

Grade: 3D, moderate day hike

Trailhead: From Chinquapin junction on the Wawona Road, drive 15.5 miles up the Glacier Point to its end. **D1.**

Introduction: This hike, the Pohono Trail, takes you past several excellent viewpoints, each showing a different part of Yosemite Valley in a unique perspective. After early June carry enough water (usually one quart) to last until midpoint, Bridalveil Creek, which is the hike's only permanent source of water.

Description: From the extreme east end of the Glacier Point parking lot, we start south up a trail that in a minute forks. **Day Hike 18** branches left but we branch right and under white-fir cover cross the Glacier Point Road in another minute. Beyond it we immediately branch right again since the path ahead climbs to a ranger's residence. Our still-climbing trail curves west up to a switchback, then south to a road. This we cross and continue up the relentless grade to a north-descending crest which we cross before climbing briefly south to a gully. In it, almost a mile from Glacier Point, we are faced with a choice. Our route, the Pohono Trail, goes west to the brink of Sentinel Fall—usually dry by midsummer— while the alternate route, which starts north before climbing south, goes to scenic Sentinel Dome. Should you take the dome route, you can return to the Pohono Trail or you can take a more level route that adds ⅔ mile to your total distance. From the dome you follow **Day Hike 15** in reverse, then the first half of **Day Hike 14**, which takes you back to the Pohono Trail.

Our main route, the Pohono Trail, leaves the gully, traverses southwest across a lower face of Sentinel Dome, then drops to a gravelly gully whose north-side sediments are part of a moraine that marked the top of a glacier that once filled Yosemite Valley. These sediments stay with us along our short, sometimes steep descent to Sentinel Creek. Paralleling its bank we can walk 90 yards out to a point where we get our first good Valley views since Glacier Point. Those hiking before mid-June will also see upper Sentinel Fall splashing down a chute immediately west of the point.

Beyond the sometimes stagnant creek we climb past lodgepole pines and white firs, then, before a crest junction, past Jeffrey pines and red firs. At the junction we rejoin the alternate route and, as in the second half of **Day Hike 14**, descend a trail to the Fissures and Taft Point. Be careful when exploring this scenic though precipitous area. From the westernmost fissure the Pohono Trail descends south, then contours west to a low ridge. By following the ridge about 250 yards out to its end you'll reach an unnamed viewpoint that gives you a view down upon the Cathedral Rocks, lined up in a row. Descending from the low ridge, the shady Pohono Trail drops 700 feet to a bridge over Bridalveil Creek, on whose south bank you'll find the hike's only fair campsite, nestled under lodgepole pines.

From the creek, which is our hike's approximate midpoint, we climb west to two junctions with a lateral trail. This lateral climbs 2

miles south to the Glacier Point Road, then a short mile beyond it to
Bridalveil Campground. This lateral trail constitutes the first half of
Hike 13 (described in the northern direction), and turning to the
second half of that hike's description, we let it guide us over to
Dewey Point. West from that point we follow **Hike 12,** described in
the reverse direction, down to Discovery View, at the east end of
Wawona Tunnel.

Day Hike 17
Glacier Point to Yosemite Valley via Four Mile Trail

Distance: 4.5 miles (7.2 km) one way
Grade: 1A, easy 2-hour hike
Trailhead: Same as for Day Hike 16. **D1.**
Introduction: This trail provides a very scenic, enjoyable descent
to Yosemite Valley—a descent that will acquaint you with the
Valley's main features. This descent also gives you a feel for the
Valley's 3000-foot depth.
Description: Before building the Yosemite Falls trail (**Day Hike
10**) John Conway first worked on this trail, completing it in 1872.
Originally about 4 miles long, it was rebuilt and lengthened in 1929
but the trail's name stuck. Our trail starts west from the north side of
a snack shop, and we enter a cool bowl whose shady white firs and
sugar pines usually harbor snow patches well into June. Contouring
northwest, we eventually emerge from forest shade and, looking
east, can see Glacier Point's two overhanging rocks capping a
vertical wall. Soon we curve west, veer in and out of a cool gully,
then reach a descending ridge. On it, views of Sentinel Rock provide
a good gauge to mark our downward progress.
    Brush dominates the first dozen switchback legs, thereby giving
us unobstructed panoramas, though making the hike a hot one for
anyone ascending from the Valley floor on a summer afternoon.
However, as we duck east into a gully, shady conifers appear,

though they somewhat censor our views. About midway down the series of switchbacks, gold-cup oaks begin to compete with white firs and Douglas-firs, and our view is obstructed even more. After descending ⅔ the vertical distance to the Valley floor, our switchbacks temporarily end. A long steady descent now ensues, mostly past gold-cup oaks, though black oaks and incense-cedars also appear. After ¼ mile we cross a creeklet that usually flows until early July and near its lush vegetation we get an excellent view down at Leidig Meadow.

Our steady descent again enters oak cover and we skirt below the base of imposing but largely hidden Sentinel Rock. At last a final group of switchbacks carry us down to an abandoned parking loop, closed in about 1975, and we proceed north, intersecting the Valley floor's southside trail, **Day Hike 2,** halfway to our end point, the eastbound road.

Day Hike 18
Glacier Point to Yosemite Valley via Nevada and Vernal Falls

Distance: 9.1 miles (14.6 km) one way

Grade: 2C, moderate day hike

Trailhead: Same as for Day Hike 16. **D1.**

Introduction: Of all the trails one could take down to the floor of Yosemite Valley, this one is the most scenic. Either take a bus up to Glacier Point or have a friend drop you there and meet you at Camp Curry, down in the Valley.

Description: Our trail starts on the highly scenic crest beside the east end of the Glacier Point parking lot and climbs to a fork. The Pohono Trail, **Day Hike 16,** veers right, but we veer left, climbing a bit more before starting a moderate descent. A switchback leg helps ease the grade, then we descend, usually without views, through a predominantly red-fir forest that has some Jeffrey pines and a smattering of white firs, sugar pines and black oaks. A 1987 fire blackened most of the forest from the trailhead to just beyond the upcoming Buena Vista Trail junction, but most of the trees survived. Between charred trunks, great views occasionally appear of Half Dome, Mt. Broderick, Liberty Cap, Nevada Fall and Mt. Starr King. After 1⅔ miles and an 800-foot drop, our Glacier Point-Panorama Trail meets the Buena Vista Trail. In 2.2 miles this heads up-canyon to Illilouette Creek, then leads up along it to intersect the Mono Meadow Trail (**Backpack Hike 4**).

Our trail branches left and switchbacks down to a spur trail that goes down a few yards to a railing. Here, atop an overhanging cliff, we get an unobstructed view of 370-foot-high Illilouette Fall, which splashes down over a low point on the rim of massive, joint-controlled Panorama Cliff. Behind it Half Dome rises boldly toward the heavens while above Illilouette Creek Mt. Starr King rises even higher. In ¼ mile our trail descends to a wide bridge upstream from one washed out in the '50s. From the bridge and its dangerously slippery slabs we face a major climb up along the rim of Panorama Cliff. First we pass above the brink of Illilouette Fall, then we gently ascend northeast along the brushy rim. Our ascending trail quickly veers away from the rim to switchback up a gully, then returns to it at Panorama Point. Here we have a scenic view that is surpassed by another one about ⅓ mile up the trail. From it you have a panorama extending from Upper Yosemite Fall east past Royal Arches, Washington Column and North Dome to Half Dome.

Our forested, moderate climb ends after 200 more feet of elevation gain, and then we descend gently to the rim for some more views, contour east, and absorb even more views, dominated by Half Dome, Mt. Broderick, Liberty Cap, Clouds Rest and Nevada Fall. Our contour ends at a junction with the Mono Meadow Trail, which climbs southwest over a low ridge before descending to Illilouette Creek.

Beyond the junction a major, mile-long descent ensues, dropping us via many switchbacks through a generally viewless forest to a trail fork, from where each branch descends but a few yards to the

John Muir Trail. To complete your hike, descend west along this scenic, view-packed trail, but not until you've first walked over to the brink of roaring Nevada Fall. The descent along the John Muir Trail is described in the last part of **Day Hike 20.**

Alternately, you could descend the Mist Trail, a shorter route, which begins a few hundred yards northeast of Nevada Fall. Being shorter, it is also steeper, and is potentially dangerous for those who try to descend it too rapidly. This wet route is described in the opposite direction in the first part of **Day Hike 20.** From the reunion of the John Muir and the Mist trails, you walk but a minute to the Vernal Fall bridge, then follow **Day Hike 19** in reverse down to the Happy Isles shuttle-bus stop. From it you can ride or walk west to Camp Curry, the Valley's east hub of activity.

Day Hike 19
Vernal Fall Bridge

Distance: 1.6 miles (2.6 km) round trip

Grade: 1A, moderate 2-hour hike

Trailhead: Happy Isles shuttle-bus stop in eastern Yosemite Valley. **D1.**

Introduction: Of all the Park's hikes this one—along a broad, paved path—is the most popular. If you have time for only one short hike, this is the one to take.

Description: From the shuttle-bus stop you head south across a shady flat to the Happy Isles area, which has the informative Happy Isles Trail Center. By a curio shop you cross a bridge, and at its east end reach a gaging station. From this station the famous John Muir Trail heads about 210 miles southward to the summit of Mt. Whitney. After a few minutes up it we meet a trail on our right that descends to upper Happy Isle. In a few more yards we reach a small cistern with refreshing mountain water. Beyond it the climb south steepens, and before bending east we get a glance back at Upper Yosemite Fall, partly blocked by the nearby Glacier Point Apron.

This smooth, curved apron contrasts with the generally angular nature of Yosemite topography. Scanning the canyon wall south of the apron you'll see a series of oblique-angle cliffs—all of them remarkably similar in orientation since they've fractured along the same series of joint planes. At the canyon's end Illilouette Fall plunges 370 feet over a vertical, joint-controlled cliff. Just east of the fall is a large scar which marks the site of a major rockfall that broke loose during the winter of 1968–69.

Climbing east we head up a severely glaciated canyon, one that in times past was buried by as much as 3500 feet of glacier ice. Hiking beneath the unstable, highly fractured south wall of Sierra Point, we cross a talus slope—an accumulation of rockfall boulders. The May 1980 Mammoth Lakes earthquake set up three rockfalls here, which finally occurred in conjunction with heavy rains in late spring 1986. Entering forest shade once more, we first struggle up the steep trail before making a quick drop to our destination, the Vernal Fall bridge. From it we see Vernal Fall—a broad wall of green-white water—plunge 320 feet over a vertical cliff before cascading toward us. Looming above the fall are two glacier-trimmed masses, Mt. Broderick (left) and Liberty Cap (right). Just beyond our bridge you'll find restrooms and an emergency telephone. **Day Hike 20** continues the description up-canyon.

Day Hike 20
Vernal-Nevada Falls Loop

Distance: 5.9 miles (9.5 km) semiloop trip

Grade: 2D, strenuous half-day hike

Trailhead: Happy Isles shuttle-bus stop in eastern Yosemite Valley. **D1.**

Introduction: Mile for mile, this very popular hike may be the most scenic one in the Park. The first part of this loop goes up the famous (or infamous) Mist Trail—a steep, strenuous trail that sprays you with Vernal Fall's mist. Take a poncho or other rain gear or, if it is a warm day, strip down to swimwear, for you can dry out on the sun-drenched rocks above the fall. For the best photos start after 10 a.m.

Description: The previous hike tells you what to see along your hike up to the Vernal Fall bridge. About 200 yards beyond the bridge we come to the start of our loop. Here the Mist Trail continues upriver while the John Muir Trail starts a switchbacking ascent to the right. This is the route taken by mules and horses. We'll go up the Mist Trail and down the John Muir Trail. You can, of course, go up or down either, but by starting the loop up the Mist Trail, you stand less chance of an accident. Hikers are more apt to slip or twist an ankle descending than ascending, and the Mist Trail route to Nevada Fall has ample opportunity for such a mishap.

In swim suit or rain gear we start up the Mist Trail and soon, rounding a bend, receive our first spray. If you're climbing this trail on a sunny day, you're almost certain to see one, if not two, rainbows come alive in the fall's spray. The spray increases as we advance toward the fall, but we get a brief respite behind a large boulder. Beyond it we complete our 300-odd steps, most of them wet, which guide us up through a verdant, spray-drenched garden. We struggle up the last few dozen steps under the shelter of trees, then, reaching an alcove beneath an ominous overhang, scurry left up a last set of stairs. These, protected by a railing, guide us to the top of a vertical cliff. Pausing here we can study our route, the nearby fall, and the river gorge. Our railing ends just upriver from the brink of Vernal Fall. It is there for a reason. Every year several people are swept over the Park's falls because they ignore warnings.

Plunging into the upper end of chilly Emerald Pool is churning Silver Apron. Late in the summer when the Merced's flow is noticeably down, one is tempted to glide down this watery chute into Emerald Pool. This is hazardous, for one can easily crash on some boulders just beyond the end of this silvery chute. Rivers are not to be taken lightly. You'll see a bridge spanning the narrow gorge that confines the Silver Apron, and this structure is our immediate goal. The trail can be vague in our area for so many paths have been trampled through it, but our route leaves the river near the east end of Emerald Pool, climbs briefly south, then angles east to a nearby junction. From it a view-packed trail climbs almost ½ mile to Clark Point, where it meets the John Muir Trail. We, however, stay low and curve left over to the bridge spanning the Silver Apron. Beyond it we have a short, moderate climb up to a broad bench which was once the site of La Casa Nevada. Opened in 1870 it was managed by Albert Snow until 1891, when a fire burned the main structure to the ground. Today one can find outhouses in this area.

Spurred onward by the sight and sound of plummeting Nevada Fall, we climb eastward, soon commencing a series of more than two dozen compact switchbacks. As we ascend them, Nevada Fall slips out of view, but we can still see towering Liberty Cap. Our climb ends at the top of a joint-controlled gully where, on brushy slopes, we once again meet the John Muir Trail. From this junction we head southwest toward nearby Nevada Fall. Along this stretch you may notice knobby boulders—rich in feldspar crystals—that contrast strongly with the bedrock they lie on. These boulders are *erratics*—that is, rocks left by retreating glaciers which were here perhaps as recently as 10,000 years ago. Nearing the Merced River you may also notice patches of bedrock that have been polished, striated and gouged by a former glacier.

Just a few yards before the Nevada Fall bridge you can strike northwest on a short, easily missed spur trail down to a viewpoint beside the fall's brink. This viewpoint's railing is seen from the fall's bridge, thereby giving you an idea where the trail ends. Don't go straying along the cliff's edge and, as mentioned earlier, respect the river—it too often sweeps people over the fall. Standing near the tumultuous brink of the Merced River, you can look across its glaciated canyon to distant Glacier Point. Vernal Fall, which lies just beyond Emerald Pool, plunges over a vertical wall that is perpendicular to the one that Nevada Fall plunges over. This part of the Merced River canyon is bounded by major fracture planes, or joint planes, which account for the canyon's angular landscape.

From the Nevada Fall bridge we strike southwest, immediately passing more glacier polish and erratic boulders as well as an outhouse, off in the trees. Our short, gentle climb ends at a junction just beyond a seeping spring, where we meet the Glacier Point-

Liberty Cap and 594-foot-high Nevada Fall

Panorama trail. Folks descending from Glacier Point (**Day Hike 18**) join us here for a descent to Happy Isles along the John Muir Trail. This Muir Trail segment starts with a high traverse that provides an ever-changing panorama of domelike Liberty Cap and broad-topped Mt. Broderick. As we progress west, Half Dome comes into prominence, its hulking mass vying for our attention. Eventually we descend to Clark Point, where we meet a scenic lateral trail that switchbacks down to Emerald Pool.

Backpackers and those wishing to keep dry continue down the John Muir Trail, which curves south into a gully, switchbacks down to the base of spreading Panorama Cliff, then switchbacks down a talus slope. Largely shaded by gold-cup oaks and Douglas-firs, it reaches a junction with a horse trail—no hikers allowed—that descends to the Valley's stables. We continue a brief minute more to a junction with the Mist Trail, turn left and quickly arrive at the Vernal Fall bridge. From it Happy Isles is a brief 15-minute descent.

Day Hike 21
Half Dome via Little Yosemite Valley

Distance: 16.4 miles (26.4 km) round trip

Grade: 4E, strenuous day hike

Trailhead: Happy Isles shuttle-bus stop in eastern Yosemite Valley. **D1.**

Introduction: Half Dome "is a crest of granite rising to the height of 4,737 feet above the Valley, perfectly inaccessible, being probably the only one of all the prominent points about the Yosemite which never has been and never will be trodden by human foot." So wrote Josiah D. Whitney—California's first prominent geologist—in his 1870 *Yosemite Guide-Book.* Just five years later the impossible was accomplished, when George Anderson labored for weeks drilling a row of holes up to the "inaccessible" summit, reached on the 12th of October, 1875. Today, hundreds if not thousands of visitors reach the summit every year, climbing a frightening cable stairway that lies close to the original ascent route.

Description: Follow **Day Hike 20** up the Mist Trail or John Muir Trail to a junction just northeast of the brink of Nevada Fall. From this junction we climb up a brushy gully, then quickly descend into forest cover and reach the Merced River. Beneath pines, firs and incense-cedars we continue northeast along the river's azalea-lined bank, then quickly encounter a trail fork. The left fork climbs and then descends the low east ridge of Liberty Cap. It is a "shortcut" to the Half Dome Trail, but the amount of climbing it requires offsets the little distance you'll save on it. We keep right on the main trail, and go a short half mile to another junction, from where the John Muir Trail/Half Dome Trail branches north while the Merced Lake Trail continues east. Just east of this junction you're likely to find a summer ranger who can give you advice on where to camp, how to bear-bag your food, where to find the outhouse, and what sights to see. Many hikers on their way to Half Dome or Merced Lake (**Backpack Hike 1**) spend their first night here. In ¼ mile you rejoin the "shortcut" route and begin a steady, unrelenting climb to the base of the dome's cables. After 1⅓ miles of forested ascent you leave the John Muir Trail, which climbs east to Tuolumne Meadows, and you continue up the Half Dome Trail.

After 0.6 mile of ascent we meet a spur trail that goes about 280 yards east to a spring—your last opportunity for water. The trail bends west before reaching a saddle, and it then climbs through a forest of red firs and Jeffrey pines instead of white firs and incense-cedars. Half Dome's northeast face comes into view and, topping a crest, we get a fine view of Clouds Rest and its satellites, the Quarter Domes.

A crest traverse reveals more views, then it ends all too soon at the base of Half Dome's shoulder, where a sign warns us of the potential lightning hazard. Even when thunderstorms are miles away, static electricity can build up on the summit. Out of a clear blue sky a charge can bolt down the cable, throwing your arms off it—or worse. If your hair starts standing on end, beat a hasty retreat!

Almost two dozen short switchbacks guide us up the view-packed ridge of the dome's shoulder and, near the top, a cable lends

Hikers descending Half Dome's intimidating cable route

additional aid. A real danger on this section is loose gravel, which could prove fatal to a careless hiker. Topping the shoulder we are confronted with the famous, intimidating Half Dome cables. (The cables are put up in mid-May and removed in early October in a normal year.) The ascent starts out gently enough, but it too quickly steepens almost to a 45° angle. On this stretch, first-timers often slow to a snail's pace, clenching both cables with sweaty hands.

The rarefied air certainly hinders our progress as we struggle upward, but an easing gradient gives new incentive and soon we are scrambling up to the broad summit area. About the size of 17 football fields, it provides quite an area to explore. With caution most hikers proceed to the dome's high point (8842'), located at the north end, from where they can view the dome's overhanging northwest point. A few stout-hearted souls actually peer over the lip of this overhanging point for a super-frightening view down the dome's 2000-foot face. To non-climbers it is hard to imagine that anyone could climb such a face, yet it has been climbed on hundreds of occasions and by several different routes.

From the broad summit of this granodiorite monolith you have a 360° panorama. You can look down Yosemite Valley to the bald brow of El Capitan and up Tenaya Canyon past Clouds Rest to Cathedral Peak, the Sierra crest and Mt. Hoffmann. Mt. Starr King—a dome that rises only 250 feet above us—dominates the Illilouette Creek basin to the south, while the Clark Range cuts the sky to the southeast. Looking due east across the summit of Moraine Dome, one sees Mt. Florence, whose broad form hides Mt. Lyell, behind it.

Day Hike 22
Alder Creek Trail to Bishop Creek

Distance: 6.3 miles (10.2 km) round trip
Grade: 2C, moderate half-day hike
Trailhead: On the Wawona Road 3.9 miles north of the Wawona Campground entrance and 280 yards west of the Alder Creek

crossing; also 7.4 miles south of the Glacier Point Road junction.
B4.

Introduction: Your descent to Bishop Creek can be one of the Sierra's most pleasant springtime hikes, though by early summer the creeks run dry and temperatures soar. Most of this trail's length is across rolling topography carpeted with mountain misery; nowhere else in the Park will you see such a spread of this low, lightly scented sbrub.

Description: From the road's bend near a cut through weathered granite, our trail drops below the Wawona Road and parallels it northwest. The trail quickly widens along an abandoned road, which it momentarily leaves. After about ½ mile of traversing, it begins a long drop to the South Fork Merced River. About 1.2 miles from our trailhead, we leave the Park and in the Sierra National Forest descend 0.8 mile to a springtime creek. In a short ¼ mile beyond it we climb to a low ridge, on which you'll find about a half dozen Indian mortar holes, perhaps covered with black-oak leaves, just a few yards west of the trail. From the ridge we have a steady descent, one that winds in and out of gullies as it drops about 550 feet to the banks of Bishop Creek. From there you could continue down to the South Fork Merced River, which involves a total drop of almost 800 feet along a dry, steep 1.4-mile course. However, the steepness, heat, riverside trash and springtime ticks make the descent not worth it.

Day Hike 23
Chilnualna Fall

Distance: 8.1 miles (13.0 km) round trip

Grade: 2D, moderate day hike

Trailhead: At the end of the Chilnualna Road. The Chilnualna Road starts immediately north of the bridge across the South Fork Merced River, near Wawona. On it you drive past the Pioneer

Yosemite History Center and a nearby fork right to the Park's district office. In a few hundred yards you'll reach the signed Alder Creek Trail, ½ mile along your road. Then, in 1⅓ miles, at the east end of North Wawona, the Chilnualna Road ends above its namesake, Chilnualna Creek. Another road, branching left from Chilnualna Road at "The Redwoods," parallels our road to this end point, the start of the foot trail. If you are taking horses you should start at another trailhead. Branch left on this higher road and follow it ¼ mile to an intersection with a paved road. Turn left and drive ⅓ mile up to its second switchback. From it a horse trail climbs 280 yards east to the end of the foot trail. Park at this switchback or at the road's end, about 150 yards farther. **C4-C5.**

Introduction: Although glaciers may have descended Chilnualna Creek, they were probably few in number and played a minimal role in carving the lower Chilnualna Creek canyon. Hence, Chilnualna Fall, like Feather Fall in the extreme northwestern Sierra Nevada, is largely the product of stream processes. It gives the hiker an idea of what some of the Yosemite Valley falls may have looked like before glaciation.

Description: Our foot trail starts within earshot of dashing Chilnualna Creek and climbs steeply almost to the creek's 25-foot high fall. From this point our trail, overshadowed by a low, vertical cliff, climbs even more steeply than before, soon reaching a junction with the horse trail. Continuing upward from it, we cross a manzanita-decked ridge, then enter a forest of ponderosa pines and incense-cedars. On this ascent a few breaks in the vegetation allow us to survey the Wawona area to the south, Wawona Point to the southeast and Wawona Dome to the east. Climbing east we reach Chilnualna Creek in a few minutes, then briefly follow it up-canyon. Where the trail bends away from the creek, make sure you have enough water to last until the campsites above Chilnualna Fall, almost 3 miles farther. In mid and late summer the ascent can be hot and dry.

On a moderately graded trail we now climb more than a dozen switchbacks of various lengths up into a cooler forest before making a fairly open traverse southeast toward Chilnualna Fall. On it we see the entire length of the fall, which churns for hundreds of feet down a deep, confining chute. Our trail comes to within a few yards of the fall's brink, but due to loose gravel and lack of protective railing, you should not venture any closer to it.

Not far above Chilnualna Fall is an upper fall, a 60-foot-high cascade that is quite impressive in early season. To get around this fall and its small gorge, our trail switchbacks north, then curves south above the lip of the gorge. Views extending over the forested Wawona area are left behind as we reach a trail junction. Just below this junction and also below the main trail east of it, you'll find several good campsites. From the junction **Backpack Hike 5** follows the trail climbing northeast up Chilnualna Creek, while **Backpack Hike 2** follows the trail descending south from Turner Meadows.

Day Hike 24
Wawona to Mariposa Grove

Distance: 13.0 miles (20.9 km) round trip

Grade: 3D, moderate day hike

Trailhead: Several. Park at Wawona Hotel, at the store north of the hotel, or at the Pioneer Yosemite History Center. **B5.**

Introduction: Though most visitors drive to the Mariposa Grove, one can also walk to it. This hike describes the forested pathway to the Mariposa Grove of Big Trees, or Wawona, as the Indians used to call them.

Description: Regardless of where you start in the Wawona area, you shouldn't have much trouble finding the trailhead. A north-south road cuts across a low crest along the east side of the Wawona structures, and just north of the actual crest, a trail, signed the *Two Hour Ride Trail*, climbs east from the road. On this dusty horse trail we quickly pass an old, abandoned canal, climb to the crest, and in a short mile from the trailhead reach a crest fork. To the left, a broad horse path descends to a summer camp. From it the broad horse path climbs southeast back up to a junction with our trail. This junction is reached after a second short mile of dusty trail hiking, most of it right along the forested crest. Views of large Wawona meadow are generally poor or nonexistent.

From the saddle where the broad horse path rejoins our trail, we turn south, briefly descend to a point a stone's throw from the noisy, paved Wawona Road, and parallel it an equally brief distance east to a junction. Here the Two Hour Ride Trail leaves us, crossing the nearby highway to return to the Wawona area. Now on a less used route, we climb east up a steepening ridge before veering south on our 1⅔-mile ascent to a usually flowing creek.

Our trail maintains its moderate gradient as it climbs south above the headwalls of two eroding, enlarging bowls. Then in ½ mile it begins to switchback up to a broad-crest junction with a ridge trail. If you intend to follow **Day Hike 25,** you'll end it at this junction, then descend the way you came back to Wawona. The combined length of Day Hikes 24 and 25 is 17.5 miles (28.2 km)—a strenuous 4D day hike.

Now merged, Day Hikes 24 and 25 follow a rolling, wandering trail a long ½ mile southeast to a junction, from which you could continue your traverse an equal distance to the tunneled California Tree and the enormous Grizzly Giant. Rather, we turn right and on a switchbacking trail descend an equal distance to the upper (northeast) end of the Mariposa Grove parking lot. After walking through it you'll reach the turnaround point of **Day Hike 24**—an information kiosk—from which **Day Hike 25** begins. Along it you'll thoroughly explore the giant sequoias and their interesting natural history.

Day Hike 25
Mariposa Grove of Big Trees

Distance: 6.9 miles (11.0 km) loop trip; other, shorter loops possible

Grade: 2C, moderate half-day hike

Trailhead: From the Park's south entrance station drive east 2.1 miles up to road's end at the Big Trees parking lot. **C5.**

Introduction: Near the southwest end of the parking lot is an information kiosk in which visitors can get introduced to the Mariposa Grove while waiting to take the tram. The tram ride gives you an instructive, guided tour of the grove's salient features and, where it stops, you can get off, explore the immediate area, then get on the next tram. However, by hiking from the kiosk rather than riding a tram from it, one gets a more intimate experience with the giant sequoia and associated plants and animals.

Description: Our path, signed the *Mariposa Grove Foot Trails,* starts eastward up along a quiet, azalea-lined creeklet that drains the shady slopes. Judging from this environment, one would conclude that sequoias are shade-loving trees. However, extensive research showed that the very opposite is true; abundant sunlight is important in every stage of the tree's development. The tree, growing at 1–2 feet per year, is in a race to the sky with competing conifers. Only when it reaches the 200-foot mark—after about 150 years—is it more or less assured of extreme longevity.

The giant's race toward the sun begins at the very start—with the seeds. A mature giant sequoia can produce 300–400,000 seeds in a year and more than a *half billion* if it lives to a ripe old age. Why then doesn't a grove of sequoias "plant all the mountain ranges in the world?" The giant sequoia is a classic example of reproductive fragility. Of paramount importance is the tree's access to sufficient soil moisture during the growing season. This is especially true for the seed and seedling.

Realizing that extremely few sequoia seeds give rise to mature sequoias, we continue on our walk away from the grove's information kiosk. Our shady trail gives rise to a short path that crosses our trailside, azalea-lined creeklet to reach the adjacent tram road. We take a second path, about 250 yards from the start of our trail, and walk a few paces over to the Fallen Monarch, a huge, downed sequoia lying beside the road. Just how long it has lain "in state" is anybody's guess. A sequoia such as the Fallen Monarch can resist decay for 20 centuries or more. Unlike its thin, outer sapwood, the tree's heartwood is *almost* immune to fire, insect and fungal attack.

A giant-sequoia cone, ⅔ life size

Since our short path to the Fallen Monarch ends near the tree's roots, you might take a look at them. Note how shallow they are. These shallow roots are the sequoia's "Achilles' heel," for though the mature tree is usually immune to almost any kind of attack, it is likely—especially in old age—to be toppled during a violent windstorm. Near the uphill end of the Fallen Monarch, the Pillars of Heaven Nature Trail begins from the tram road's south side and climbs northeast before uniting with our main route—an old road. Along the nature trail you'll see that fire can damage a sequoia, though one rarely destroys it. Since debris piles up on *any* tree's upslope side, that is the side that is likely to burn with the greatest intensity in a ground fire. One fire may hardly damage a sequoia's bark, which is fire-resistant because it is soft and fibrous and contains very little pitch. A dozen or more fires, however, can do extensive damage, as we'll see along our hike.

From the north end of the nature trail our main trail, an old stage road, climbs about 200 yards to a crossing of the paved tram road. Here, near the Bachelor and the Three Graces, our path forks, and we go right (east) up to the Grizzly Giant. Like the Leaning Tower of Pisa, this 2500-year-old giant seems ready to fall any second and one wonders how such a top-heavy, shallow-rooted specimen could have survived as long as it has. A giant it is, ranking fifth largest among the sequoias, and having enough timber to build 20 homes. Fortunately, sequoia wood is very brittle and is not economical to log.

Heading north from the east end of the enclosure circling the Grizzly Giant, we reach the California Tree, also enclosed, in 50 yards. This sequoia, like the famous Wawona Tunnel Tree, had a deep burn in its lower trunk, which was then cut away to make a tunnel. Immediately beyond the California Tree we meet an east-west trail. By heading ¼ mile west on it you'll reach a junction with a spur trail that descends to the Bachelor and the Three Graces. By contouring another ¼ mile west, you'll reach a junction from where the trail from Wawona (**Day Hike 24**) descends south to the parking lot and kiosk. We'll return along that descent.

Walk the Sequoia woods at any time of the year and you will say they are the most beautiful and majestic on earth. Beautiful and impressive contrasts meet you everywhere—the colors of tree and flower, rock and sky, light and shade, strength and frailty, endurance and evanescence . . .

—John Muir

First, however, we still face the great bulk of our climbing as our trail immediately turns north and climbs 200 yards to a crossing of the tram road. From that road we climb almost one mile and 500 vertical feet up forested slopes to a trail junction just below the road's upper-loop section. From our junction one could ascend the Upper Loop trail as it climbs counterclockwise, paralleling the road's loop over to the Wawona Tunnel Tree. Rather, we turn left and descend a few yards northwest, meeting a trail that climbs ½ mile up from the tram road. Instead of making our 500-foot trail ascent, you could hike ⅔ mile up the tram road to a hairpin turn, then take the ½-mile trail up to our Upper Loop trail. This slightly longer alternate route has one advantage: you see the Clothespin Tree, which stands near the hairpin turn. Fire has burned away part of its lower heartwood, forming a 60-foot-high cleft that splits the tree in two like an old-fashioned clothespin.

Trees of its stature have been overestimated with regard to weight. The largest sequoia—the General Sherman in Sequoia National Park—weighs only about 450 tons, dry weight, and the Grizzly Giant weighs about 300. The reason for the tree's "light" weight is the low density of its wood; it weighs only 18 pounds per cubic foot, about ⅓ that of an oak. The giant sequoia, with its lightweight, brittle wood *needs* its wide-diameter bulk to support its mushrooming, windswept crown.

From the upper junction with the alternate route, our main trail traverses about 110 yards north to a junction with an east-west trail. Westward this trail descends a few hundred yards to the tram road, crosses it, then quickly ends at the trail we'll eventually descend on. From our junction beside the tip of a large, fallen giant, we proceed east up-trail through a spacious forest with mature sequoias to the Mariposa Grove Museum. A few yards before it another eastbound trail, on our left, merges with ours. To the west this trail forks, one branch quickly ending at our eastbound trail, while the other branch crosses a creeklet and the tram road, then goes past the closed Big Trees Lodge before ending at our eventual descent route.

Be sure to visit the museum. In it you will find information and displays on the giant sequoia, its related plants and animals, and the area's history. From the museum you can take any of four routes up to Wawona Tunnel Tree. On the tram road you can either go north,

The museum is dwarfed by giant sequoias

passing Pluto's Chimney—a dead-but-standing sequoia (a rare sight)—or you can go south, passing the Columbia Tree, which at almost 290 feet is the grove's tallest. The most direct route is a trail that climbs ⅓ mile northeast up to the Tunnel Tree. Finally, the route the author prefers starts south along the tram road, then after a few yards—just before the Columbia Tree—leaves it and heads southeast back up to the road. Along this trail stretch you'll pass the Stable Tree, a giant that fell in the *summer* of 1934. Most sequoias fall during the long, stormy winter.

Where the preferred route crosses the tram road you'll see the amazing Telescope Tree, which has been hollowed out by fire. Inside it you can look straight up to the heavens. Despite its great internal loss, this tree is still very much alive for its vital fluids—as in all trees—are conducted in the sapwood, immediately beneath the bark. The heartwood is just dead sapwood whose main function is support. The Telescope Tree, with its hollow interior, is a good candidate for blowdown.

From the back side of the tree our trail climbs 35 yards to the Upper Loop trail, which we then follow ⅓ mile counterclockwise over to the Wawona Tunnel Tree. During the late winter or spring of 1969 this 2200-year-old giant fell, after bearing 88 years of tourist traffic. Originally fire-scarred like other giants, it was tunneled through in 1881 to provide stagecoach riders with a thrill of a lifetime—riding *through* a tree.

After examination of this downed giant, continue north on the Upper Loop trail or the tram road to a nearby crest saddle. Just 40 yards east of it is the Galen Clark Tree, a fine specimen named for the man who first publicized this grove and later became its guardian. The Upper Loop trail crosses the saddle at a road junction, and before we descend along it we first angle right and follow the crest road ¼ mile up to Wawona Point. No giant sequoias are found along this road, probably because of insufficient ground water. At the point we see the large, partly man-made meadow at Wawona, to the northwest, and the long, curving cliff of Wawona Dome, breaking a sea of green, to the north.

After returning to the crest saddle, we descend west along the Upper Loop trail. About ⅔ mile from the saddle our trail gives rise to a wide path that departs south down to the close-by Big Trees Lodge. Near this path junction we see the first giant sequoia since the Galen Clark Tree, and will see more farther down. In a few minutes we come to a second junction, and here the Upper Loop trail branches left to quickly cross the tram road. We curve right and drop about 470 feet along a moderate, short-mile descent to a junction with **Day Hike 24,** climbing 5.0 miles up from the east end of the Wawona complex. As in that hike we follow a rambling trail a long ½ mile southeast to a junction, turn right, and make a shady, moderate descent back to the parking lot and its information kiosk— our starting point.

Backpack Hike 1
Merced Lake via Little Yosemite Valley

Distance: 27.4 miles (44.1 km) round trip via John Muir and Merced Lake trails

Grade: 5E, moderate 3-day hike

Trailhead: Happy Isles shuttle-bus stop in eastern Yosemite Valley. **D1.**

Introduction: Best done in three days with overnight stops at Little Yosemite Valley and Merced Lake, this hike is often done in two by energetic weekend hikers. Its route—up a fantastic river canyon—is hard to beat anywhere in the Sierra Nevada. Although over half the route lies off the area covered by this book's map, this popular route is too important to omit.

Description: If you are wearing a backpack, you should climb to the top of Nevada Fall by the John Muir Trail, not by the Mist Trail. **Day Hike 19** describes the route to the Vernal Fall bridge; then you follow the last part of **Day Hike 20** in reverse up the obvious route to Nevada Fall. The last 1¼ miles along this section are very scenic,

Supplementary map: the Merced River Trail. Scale: 1/62,500

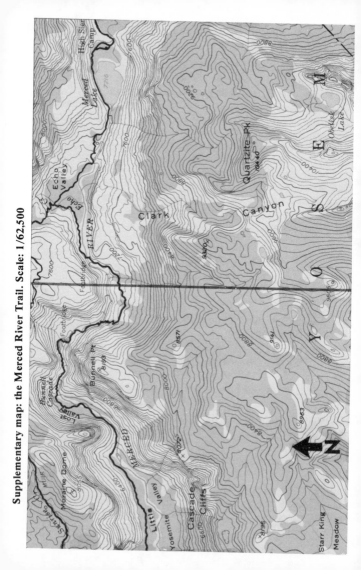

with views of Half Dome, Mt. Broderick, Liberty Cap, Nevada Fall and the Merced River canyon. Beyond the Nevada Fall bridge we soon meet the end of the Mist Trail—the short, wet, strenuous alternate route—then climb up and over into Little Yosemite Valley, described in the first paragraph of **Day Hike 21.** In its western part we leave the John Muir Trail, which veers north, then embark on a shady two-mile stroll, following the Merced Lake Trail through the broad, flat valley. The valley's floor has been largely buried by glacial sediments, which like beach sand make us work even though the trail is level. Progressing east through Little Yosemite Valley, we stay closer to the base of glacier-polished Moraine Dome than to the Merced River, and along this stretch you can branch off to riverside campsites that are far more peaceful than those near the John Muir Trail junction, which tends to be a "Grand Central Station." The valley's east end is graced by the presence of a beautiful pool—the receptacle of a Merced River cascade. Leaving the camps of the picturesque area, we climb past the cascade and glance back to see the east face of exfoliating Moraine Dome.

Our brief cascade climb heads toward the 1900-foot-high Bunnell Point cliff, which is exfoliating at such a prodigious rate that it, in stark contrast to the shiny dome opposite it, has virtually no remaining trace of glacial evidence. Rounding the base of the glacier-smoothed dome, we enter shady Lost Valley, in which no fires are allowed. At the valley's end we switchback up past Bunnell Cascade, which with the magnificent canyon scenery can easily distract us from the real danger of this exposed section of trail. Don't let the scenery carry you away.

Our up-canyon walk, which has been amazingly easy since Nevada Fall, soon reaches a series of more than a dozen switchbacks that carry us up 400 feet above the river—a route necessitated by another gorge. Our climb reaches its zenith amid a spring-fed profuse wildflower garden, bordered by aspens, which in midsummer supports a colorful array of floral species.

Beyond this glade we soon come out onto a highly polished bedrock surface. Here we can glance west and see Clouds Rest—a long ridge—standing high on the horizon. Now we descend back

Merced Lake and a view up-canyon

into tree cover and amid the white boles of quaking aspens brush through a forest carpet of bracken ferns and cross several creeklets before emerging on a bedrock bench above the river's inner gorge. From it we can study the features of a broad, hulking granitic mass opposite us whose south face is bounded by an immense arch. A "hairline" crack along its east side indicates that a major rockfall is imminent. Traversing our bench, we soon come to a bend in the river and at it bridge the Merced just above the brink of its cascades. Strolling east, we reach the west end of spacious Echo Valley—the charred site of an unnecessary holocaust—and proceed to a junction at its north edge.

Here, near an Echo Creek campsite, is the start of an alternate route you could take back to Little Yosemite Valley. But with Merced Lake our goal, we immediately bridge Echo Creek, strike southeast through burned-but-boggy Echo Valley, and climb east past the Merced River's largely unseen pools to Merced Lake's west shore. Don't camp here, but rather continue past the north shore to Merced Lake High Sierra Camp and the adjacent riverside campground, about 9¼ miles beyond the John Muir Trail junction in Little Yosemite Valley. You can count on seeing bears here, so store your food with the camp or string it high on the steel cable. The lake, being a large one at a moderate elevation, has been stocked with three species of trout: brook, brown and rainbow.

Backpack Hike 2
Bridalveil Campground-Wawona Loop

Distance: 30.3 miles (48.7 km) semiloop trip

Grade: 5E, moderate 3-day hike

Trailhead: Bridalveil Campground (see Day Hike 13 trailhead). Park at the campground's *far* end. **C2.**

Introduction: Sparkling lakes, deep canyons and alpine crests are *not* found along this hike—but then, neither are the backpacking crowds. This is a hike for those who love quiet forest trails.

Description: Gaining only about 200 feet in the first 3⅓ miles, our hike certainly starts out as one of the Park's easiest backpack trails. Although white firs and red firs are occasionally seen, they are greatly overwhelmed by a superabundance of lodgepole pines along this creekside stretch. After about 1.6 miles of it—on a ridge above nearby Bridalveil Creek—we join a trail that comes 1.7 miles from the Glacier Point Road (the **Backpack Hike 3** trailhead). A 1987 fire caused moderate damage to the forest in this vicinity. Leaving fire scars, the trail keeps above the creek for a short distance, then curves over to a moderate-sized camp along the creek's tributary. Like others we'll meet, this camp can have lots of mosquitoes before late July. A two-minute walk upstream from the camp ends at the tributary's ford, and on the east bank we meet our second junction. The lightly used, sometimes obscure trail to the left climbs a short mile east to the Ostrander Lake trail (**Backpack Hike 3**).

Turning right, we head south and climb gently for a mile to the tributary's upper basin. In it our climb becomes a moderate one and then a steep one as we struggle up to a neaby crest that separates the unglaciated Alder Creek drainage from that of the long-ago-glaciated Bridalveil Creek drainage. Jeffrey pines yield to red firs as we traverse slopes over to a junction near a saddle. The trail we'll be returning on climbs to here from Deer Camp, down to the west. Starting southeast, we quickly cross the broad saddle, enter the partly glaciated Chilnualna Creek drainage, and begin a rolling, gentle 1¼-mile descent that goes through several small meadows—all with abundant corn lilies. A few minutes before we reach the next junction, our trail touches the east edge of long Turner Meadows, and here you can make a fair camp.

At the junction we veer right, hop Turner Meadows creek, then start an unnecessary 300-foot climb up to a ridge instead of around it. On this moderate, shady ascent one has a crest view of gentle-but-glaciated Buena Vista Peak, to the east. We then make a long, 3800-foot drop to the Wawona area. On it western white pines quickly yield to their close cousins, the sugar pines, while farther down red firs yield to the closely related white firs. As this vegetative transition is taking place the sharp-eyed hiker may notice a shrubby black oak, which at about 7540 feet elevation is near the top of its altitudinal range. This oak is just past a secondary crest, and from it we plunge down to a creeklet, then make an equally long drop to its larger counterpart. From its verdant banks we have an easy ½-mile descent to a junction just above Chilnualna Creek. Here, near the confluence of this creek and its southbound tributary, you can find a suitable spot to spend your first night. You may want to first investigate Chilnualna Fall, just downstream, but be extremely careful if you do, for the rock can be treacherously slippery and there are no safety railings to keep you from being swept over the fall.

After a possibly memorable sunset and a good night's sleep, descend the trail 4.0 scenic miles to its end, following the description of **Day Hike 23** in reverse. Then, gradually descending west, walk 1⅓ miles along a road that goes through North Wawona—a private-land area within the Park. In this settlement you can get supplies, meals and lodging. Our next trail, the Alder Creek Trail, begins about ⅓ mile beyond the settlement's school, and this trailhead is just north of the Wawona District Office, which is a source of information and wilderness permits. Before resuming your loop hike, make a side trip to the nearby Pioneer Yosemite History Center, which you enter just west of a junction with the district office's spur road. By walking 200–300 yards upstream from the center's covered bridge you'll discover some small pools in the river that are among the warmest "swimming holes" found anywhere in the Park.

The signed Alder Creek Trail begins about 75 yards east of a west-heading service road. Starting north, the trail quickly turns west to make a ⅓-mile-long, diagonal climb across gullies up to a junction with a short spur trail that descends to the end of the service road. At our low elevation temperatures often soar into the 80s by early afternoon and water may be absent until we reach Alder Creek, about 6 miles from the trailhead. At the end of a 2¾-mile-long, generally viewless ascent we reach a mile-high junction, from which a steep trail descends ¾ mile to the heavily traveled Wawona Road.

Starting east, we begin a 2¾-mile rolling traverse in and out of gullies and around or over low ridges to a view of 100-foot-high Alder Creek fall below. Along the last mile or so of this section you may see railroad ties, which are the few tangible relics of a dark period in the Park's history. From the early days of World War I through the 1920s, the Yosemite Lumber Company laid railroad tracks in and around western Yosemite to log out some of the Sierra's finest stands of sugar pines.

Beyond the fall our abandoned-railroad route approaches lushly lined Alder Creek, parallels it north gently upstream for 1¼ miles, then crosses it to reach a nearby junction. Here or elsewhere along Alder Creek you can make your second night's camp. From the junction a trail climbs north 1⅓ miles to an old logging road, on which you could walk ½ mile east to the trail's resumption, which climbs a little over 3 miles to the Bridalveil Campground entrance. The thick brush—the result of logging—makes this route undesirable.

The recommended route angles right at the Alder Creek junction, immediately refords the broad creek, and then climbs east for 1¾ miles, paralleling a murmuring tributary. This white-fir-shaded stretch ends at Deer Camp, a desolate roadend flat along the south fringe of the logging area. You can camp here, though you won't find it esthetic. From the camp our trail continues east and, typical of old trails, it winds and switchbacks all too steeply up most of a 1100-

foot ascent. Midway up it, views expand, providing us with an overview of the Alder Creek basin. After about 1¼ miles of climbing, we top a crest, then momentarily descend to a trickling creeklet. Should you want to camp in this vicinity, camp at the nearby crest top, where mosquitoes are much fewer. Leaving the creeklet we climb around a meadow—rich in sedges, willows and corn lilies—then make a final short push southeast up to a junction near a saddle. From it we retrace our first day's steps 4.9 miles back to the trailhead.

Backpack Hike 3
Glacier Point Road to Ostrander Lake

Distance: 12.7 miles (20.5 km) round trip

Grade: 3C, easy 2-day hike

Trailhead: From Chinquapin junction on the Wawona Road drive 8.9 miles up the Glacier Point Road to a turnoff, on your right. This parking area is 1.3 miles past the Bridalveil Campground spur road. **C2.**

Introduction: Ostrander Lake, being the closest lake to the Glacier Point Road, is the object of many summertime weekend backpackers. It is also popular in winter and spring with cross-country skiers.

Description: The first half of our hike is easy—a gentle ascent through a forest that is interspersed with an assortment of meadows. We start along a former jeep road, and soon encounter the first of several areas of lodgepole forest badly burned in a 1987 fire. Just ⅓ mile from the trailhead we cross a sluggish creek, then amble an easy mile to a ridge junction, passing two more burned areas en route. From the ridge, a short lateral quickly drops to Bridalveil Creek—a potentially difficult June crossing—then climbs equally quickly to the Bridalveil Creek trail (Backpack Hike 2).

From the junction our jeep road contours southeast past unseen Lost Bear Meadow, leaves the burned lands, and after a mile makes a short ascent east up along a trickling creek to its crossing. Just beyond the ford our road curves west to a nearby junction with a second lateral to the Bridalveil Creek trail. Though we are now about halfway to Ostrander Lake, we've climbed very little, and from this junction we face 1,500 feet of vertical gain. Our steepening road climbs east through a mixed forest, then climbs more gently south across an open slab that provides the first views of verdant Bridalveil Creek basin. Views gradually disappear as we curve southeast into a Jeffrey-pine stand, then climb east through a shady white-fir forest. These firs are largely supplanted by red firs by the time we top a saddle that bisects Horizon Ridge. Climbing southeast up the ridge, our road passes through a generally open stretch decked with, surprisingly, sagebrush. Four hundred feet above our first saddle, the road switchbacks at a second one, then curves up to a third. From it our road makes a momentary descent southeast before bending to start a short, final ascent south. Near this bend we get far-ranging views across the Illilouette Creek basin. We can see the tops of Royal Arches and Washington Column and, above and east of them, North, Basket and Half domes. Behind Half Dome stands the Park's geographic center, broad-topped Mt. Hoffmann. Lording it over the Illilouette Creek basin is Mt. Starr King and its entourage of subsidiary domes. To the northeast the jagged crest of the Clark Range cuts the sky.

Beyond our short, final ascent south we drop in several minutes to Ostrander Hut—a ski hut used in spring by the Yosemite Natural History Association. By contacting this association—or better yet, joining it—you can get information about its Ostrander Lake Environmental Ski Tours, which explore the winter ecology of this region up to the crest of Horse Ridge, standing above our 25-acre, trout-stocked lake.

Experienced hikers can head cross-country southeast ¼ mile to a pond, then east over a ridge to a shallow bowl holding the Hart Lakes. The larger one has a rather stark granitic backdrop, the glacier-polished northeast face of Horse Ridge. After perhaps camping nearby, you can then descend northeast to the Buena Vista Trail, meeting it—if you're on course—atop the crest of a sizable moraine. If you are too low, you may end up at Edson Lake. Either head down the Buena Vista Trail and then west out the Mono Meadow Trail, for a 19.6-mile (31.6 km) loop trip, or else head up the Buena Vista Trail for more lake hunting, described in the next hike.

Backpack Hike 4
Mono Meadow to Buena Vista and Royal Arch Lakes

Distance: 30.4 miles (48.9 km) round trip

Grade: 5E, easy 4-day hike

Trailhead: From Chinquapin junction on the Wawona Road, drive 10.1 miles up Glacier Point Road to a forested saddle with a parking area, on your right. **D2.**

Introduction: The subalpine lakes nestled around Buena Vista Peak can be reached from North Wawona—Backpack Hike 5—or from three trailheads along the Glacier Point Road. This hike starts from one of these trailheads and visits five of the peak's lakes. Although this route is slightly longer than Backpack Hike 5, it requires 20 percent less climbing effort.

Description: Shaded by magnificent red firs, our trail begins with a steady, moderate descent north, followed by an easing gradient east to lodgepole-fringed Mono Meadow. Until mid-July you may face 200 yards of muddy freshets and meadow bogs before you reach the narrow meadow's east edge. During this period, desperate hikers try to circumvent the mire, and several paths may spring up to confuse you. The real trail crosses the meadow on a 120° bearing, and it becomes obvious once you're within the forest's edge.

Beyond the meadow our Mono Meadow Trail crosses a low divide, then makes a generally viewless, easy descent to a major tributary of Illilouette Creek. Here, 1½ miles from your trailhead, is your first possible campsite. We ford the tributary at the brink of some rapids, and in early season this ford could be a dangerous one. From the tributary we have a short though unnecessary climb, with 200 feet of elevation gain. The climb does have some merit, for at the crest and on our descent east from it we're rewarded with views of North, Basket and Half domes, Clouds Rest and Mt. Starr King. After a descent through a fir forest we emerge on an open slope and descend straight toward Mt. Starr King, the highest of the Illilouette Creek domes.

Immediately after the view disappears, we reach a junction with the Buena Vista Trail, which links Glacier Point with the Buena Vista Peak lakes. Turning right, we go 40 yards upcanyon to a second junction, from where our Mono Meadow Trail goes 300 yards to a usually wet ford (for hikers) of broad Illilouette Creek. Near this ford you'll find campsites—heavily visited by hikers and bears—along both banks. The trail climbing east from this vicinity takes one to some interesting domes, which provide serious challenges to climbers. The two Merced Pass Lakes, which lie up this way outside our area, are rather mediocre, and by themselves are not worth the 12¾-mile hike from the trailhead to reach them.

| God bless Yosemite bears! | —John Muir |

From our camping-area junction we now climb southeast up the Buena Vista Trail. Unfortunately, the next several miles of scenery are greatly marred from the effects of a major forest fire. In 1¼ miles we come to a creeklet with a fair camp on its west bank. Our trail's gradient gradually eases, then we cross a broad divide and in ¼ mile angle sharply left to descend along the edge of a sloping meadow. Beyond it we enter an aspen grove that hides a step-across creek. Just a few minutes' walk east of it we cross a slightly larger creek, then make a gentle ascent southeast across sandy soils to steep slopes above Buena Vista Creek. Camping is poor along the west bank, but good—and isolated—above the east bank. Fallen lodgepoles or other snags may provide access across the bouldery creek to these sites.

Soon our trail leaves Buena Vista Creek, curves southwest and climbs moderately in that direction for 1½ miles to a ford, between two meadows, of diminutive Edson Lake creek. From a poor campsite, the trail ascends along a moraine crest, then in 1 mile leaves it to angle southeast up to a higher crest. Where our trail makes a sudden angle left, you can leave it and contour ⅓ mile west over to a campsite at isolated Edson Lake. Our trail follows the higher moraine crest southwest for more than 300 yards, finally leaves the burned area, then makes a ¼-mile, view-packed descent to Hart Lakes creek. Where the trail leaves the crest, you can continue cross-country southwest along this crest, soon diagonal up slabs, then climb south up to the Hart Lakes.

From brush-lined Hart Lakes creek we make a short contour over to a second creek, this one having a small campsite on its east bank. After ½ mile of moderate ascent we cross Buena Vista Creek, which bends northeast, then continue south up a slightly shorter ascent to a recrossing of that creek. Immediately beyond we cross its western tributary, then follow this stream south briefly up to two ponds, from which we switchback up a cirque wall with ice-shattered blocks to a crest junction. **Backpack Hike 5,** ascending from North Wawona, now joins our route for a loop around the lakes of Buena Vista Peak. The first lake we encounter, about ⅓ mile southeast from the junction, is rather bleak Buena Vista Lake, stocked with rainbow and brook trout. Nestled on a broad bench at the base of the cool north slope of Buena Vista Peak, this lake is the highest and coldest one we'll see. It does, however, have two good camps.

Starting at the lake's outlet, we ascend short switchbacks up to a broad pass. From the viewless pass you can climb ¾ mile up a gentle ridge to Buena Vista Peak for an unrestricted panorama of the Park's southern area. From the pass we descend 2 easy, winding trail miles to everyone's favorite lake on this loop, Royal Arch Lake, which lies below a broad arch. This lake, like Buena Vista

Horse Ridge stands above the larger Hart Lake

Lake, is stocked with rainbow and brook trout. Just past the outlet, near the lake's southwest corner, you'll find an excellent campsite— one probably occupied by another hiker who hopes to watch the rays of the setting sun dance upon the multihued arch. For more solitude you can head cross-country ¾ mile west to less attractive Minnow Lake, stocked with brook trout.

Leaving Royal Arch Lake we parallel its outlet creek for a ½ mile, then angle south across slabs to a junction with a trail that goes first to Buck Camp (a ranger station) and then to Chiquito Pass. From the junction we descend west toward Johnson Lake, reaching good campsites along its northwest shore in just ¾ mile—with hordes of mosquitoes in early season. We don't see large Crescent Lake, but on meeting its inlet creek, about ⅓ mile beyond a meadowy divide, one can walk 150 yards downstream, passing a fair camp before reaching the lake's shallow, trout-filled waters. You might visit the lake's south end, or camp near it, for from the outlet you get a revealing view of the 2800-foot-deep South Fork Merced River canyon.

Beyond Crescent Lake's inlet creek our trail quickly turns north, passes a small creekside meadow, then climbs more than 150 feet to a second broad divide. From it we descend into the truncated headwaters of a Chilnualna Creek tributary. Our moderate-to-steep gradient ends when we approach easy-to-miss Grouse Lake. Two use trails descend about 100 yards to a fair campsite on the north shore of this shallow, reedy lakelet.

Lodgepoles and red firs monopolize the slopes along our 2-mile descent from this lake down to a hillside junction. Here, hikers completing **Backpack Hike 5** head west down-canyon to their trailhead. Hikers on the second day of that hike join us for a short northwest stretch, first up over a nearby divide, then down more than 400 feet to Chilnualna Creek. Just above its north bank is a good, medium-sized campsite, and just beyond that is another trail junction. From it **Backpack Hike 5** trekkers climb east while we traverse northwest. During midsummer, our gently ascending traverse is brightened by the orange sunbursts of alpine lilies, growing chest-high along the wetter parts of our trail. As we near Turner Meadows we encounter a trail junction from which **Backpack Hike 2** departs southwest down to the Wawona area.

Royal Arch Lake is well-named

We now backtrack along the first part of that hike, first ascending past and through a series of "Turner Meadows," then topping a forest pass to quickly meet a trail down to Deer Camp. Spurning it, we keep right, traverse to a crest and descend to a tributary of Bridalveil Creek. Before reaching that creek, however, we meet a junction, turn left and then cross the tributary. Along the tributary we momentarily pass a moderate-sized camp and in a ½ mile reach another junction. The main trail continues 1.6 miles northwest to Bridalveil Campground, but we veer right, drop to nearby Bridalveil Creek, ford it, and make an equally short climb up to the Ostrander Lake trail—a closed jeep road. In 1½ miles our northbound hike ends at the Glacier Point Road, on which we climb gently east for a half hour back to our trailhead.

Backpack Hike 5
North Wawona to Royal Arch, Buena Vista and Chilnualna Lakes

Distance: 28.3 miles (45.6 km) semiloop trip

Grade: 5E, easy 4-day hike

Trailhead: Same as the Day Hike 23 trailhead. **C4-C5.**

Introduction: Glaciers originating on the slopes of Buena Vista Peak descended north, south and west, then retreated to leave about a dozen small-to-medium lakes. This hike visits seven of these plus dashing Chilnualna Fall—one of the Park's highest falls outside Yosemite Valley.

Description: Day Hike 23 guides you up through a changing forest to campsites—a possible first night's stop—in an area around a trail junction and a south-flowing tributary of Chilnualna Creek. From that tributary our trail makes a short, steep ascent northeast, then traverses southeast. Soon reaching Chilnualna Creek, you'll find additional campsites along both its banks.

After crossing to the southeast bank, we head upstream, then veer away from the creek to make a short, moderate ascent to a low gap. Past it we enter a damp meadow—an early-season mosquito haven—then climb for a mile, paralleling the usually unseen creek at a distance before we intersect its tributary, Grouse Lake creek. Usually a jump-across creek, it can be a 20-foot wide, slippery-slab ford in late spring. Now just above 7000 feet, we feel the effects of a higher elevation as well as see them—as expressed in the predominance of stately red firs and occasional lodgepole pines. Before reaching a junction after a ¾-mile ascent, we also note our first trailside western white pines.

At the junction we join **Backpack Hike 4** for a short northwest stretch, first up over a nearby divide, then down more than 400 feet to Chilnualna Creek. Just above its north bank is a good, medium-size campsite, and just beyond that is another trail junction. Here we turn right while **Backpack Hike 4** continues ahead, bound for Turner Meadows and the Glacier Point Road.

Eastbound, we make a moderate ¼ mile ascent, followed by a gentler one that goes 1¼ miles along the lodgepole-shaded bank of Chilnualna Creek. After a ¼-mile walk along this gentler stretch, you'll find an acceptable campsite. At the end of the stretch we cross the seasonal creek that drains the middle and northern Chilnualna Lakes. We go a few yards along the larger creek that drains the southern and eastern Chilnualna Lakes, then leave it to cross a close-by bouldery ridge of a glacial moraine.

Young glacial evidence in the form of moraines, erratics and polish is often seen along the remaining 1⅔-mile, shady climb to waist-deep southern Chilnualna Lake. Being so shallow, it is one of the warmest lakes of this hiking circuit to cool off in. The best of the Chilnualna Lakes is also the least visited: the southern lake, at the base of Buena Vista Peak's western shoulder, about ½ mile east-southeast of our western lake. A more-visited lake is the middle one, which is easier to reach. From the far end of our lake, head ¼ mile up its inlet creek to a small pond, then walk due north over a low ridge to the nearby middle lake. From it one can easily regain the trail by continuing north.

Leaving our western lake and its fair west-shore campsite, we climb over a low, bouldery morainal ridge, skirt a small meadow, and cross the middle lake's ephemeral creek. Past it we curve clockwise over to the northern lake's outlet creek, parallel it upward, and then, just ¼ mile before the lake, cross over to the north bank. Upon reaching the shallow, narrow lake we find a good campsite among red firs and western white pines. If weather is threatening, camp here rather than climb east to the exposed pass.

At that 9040-foot-high pass, about a ¾-mile winding ascent from the northern lake, we meet the Buena Vista Trail. Now we follow most of the second half of **Backpack Hike 4** as it goes past Buena Vista, Royal Arch, Johnson, Crescent and Grouse lakes. You may want to visit all of them, and you should plan to spend at least a day in this scenic glacier-lake area. A little more than 2 miles west of Grouse Lake you'll leave **Backpack Hike 4** where you first met it, and descend the way you came—past Chilnualna Fall.

88

Recommended Reading

Basey, Harold E. 1976. Discovering Sierra Reptiles and Amphibians. Yosemite: Yosemite Nat. Hist. Assoc., 50 p.

Browning, Peter. 1988. Yosemite Place Names. Lafayette, CA: Great West Books, 241 p.

Beedy, Edward C., and Stephen L. Granholm. 1985. Discovering Sierra Birds. Yosemite: Yosemite Nat. Hist. Assoc., 229 p.

Calkins, Frank C., and others. 1985. Bedrock Geologic Map of Yosemite Valley, Yosemite National Park, California. Washington: U.S. Geological Survey, Map I-1639 (incl. 7 p. text).

Darvill, Fred T., Jr., M.D. 1989. Mountaineering Medicine. Berkeley: Wilderness Press, 68 p.

Gaines, David. 1988. Birds of Yosemite and the East Slope. Lee Vining, CA: Artemisia Press, 352 p.

Gibbens, Robert P., and Harold F. Heady. 1964. The Influence of Modern Man on the Vegetation of Yosemite Valley. Berkeley: Univ. of Calif. Div. of Agricultural Sciences, Manual 36, 44 p.

Grater, Russell K., and Tom A. Blaue. 1978. Discovering Sierra Mammals. Yosemite: Yosemite Nat. Hist. Assoc., 174 p.

Harvey, H. Thomas, Howard S. Shellhammer and Ronald E. Stecker. 1980. Giant Sequoia Ecology: Fire and Reproduction. Washington: Nat. Park Service, Scientific Monograph Series No. 12, 182 p.

Huber, N. King. 1987. The Geologic Story of Yosemite National Park. Washington: U.S. Geological Survey, Bulletin 1595, XII + 68 p.

Jameson, E.W., Jr., and Hans J. Peeters. California Mammals. Berkeley: Univ. of Calif. Press, Calif. Nat. Hist. Guide 52, 403 p.

Robertson, David. 1984. West of Eden: A History of the Art and Literature of Yosemite. Yosemite and Berkeley: Yosemite Nat. Hist. Assoc. and Wilderness Press, 174 p.

Rowell, Galen A., ed. 1974. The Vertical World of Yosemite. Berkeley: Wilderness Press, 207 p.

Russell, Carl P. 1968 (1976). 100 Years in Yosemite. Yosemite: Yosemite Nat. Hist. Assoc., 210 p.

Schaffer, Jeffrey P. 1977. "Pleistocene Lake Yosemite and the Wisconsin glaciation of Yosemite Valley." California Geology, v. 30, p. 243–248.

Schaffer, Jeffrey P. 1986. Yosemite Valley topographic map and text. Berkeley: Wilderness Press.

Schaffer, Jeffrey P. 1983. Yosemite National Park; A Natural-History Guide to Yosemite and Its Trails. Berkeley: Wilderness Press, 274 p.

Storer, Tracy I., and Robert L. Usinger. 1964. Sierra Nevada Natural History. Berkeley: Univ. of Calif. Press, 374 p.

Weeden, Norman F. 1986. A Sierra Nevada Flora. Berkeley: Wilderness Press, 406 p.

Whitney, Stephen. 1979. A Sierra Club Naturalist's Guide to the Sierra Nevada. San Francisco: Sierra Club Books, 526 p.

Index